ARTIST'S LIFE

Leonardo

Enrica Crispino

Leonardo

GIUNTI

Frontispiece:
Annunciation (1475-1480), detail,
Florence, Uffizi Gallery.

Many thanks to Carlo Pedretti
for his kind assistance
and invaluable suggestions. (E. C.)

Editorial Manager
Claudio Pescio

Editor
Dario Dondi

Editorial Assistant
Claudia Grisanti

Translation
Catherine Frost

Graphics and cover
Paola Zacchini

Iconographic research
Cristina Reggioli

www.leonardonline.eng
www.giunti.it

First edition: April 2007
New revised edition: February 2010

First revised reprint: July 2017

Note
Leonardo's manuscripts and drawings, all available
in the Edizione Nazionale Vinciana (Giunti),
are found in the following places:

Codex Atlanticus
in the Biblioteca Ambrosiana, Milan;

the Anatomical manuscripts and other drawings
in the Royal Library, Windsor Castle;

Codex Arundel 263 in the British Library, London;

Forster Mss. I-III
in the Victoria and Albert Museum, London;

Madrid Mss. I and II
in the Biblioteca Nacional de España, Madrid;

Manuscripts A-M
in the Library of the Institut de France, Paris;

Codex Hammer (formerly Codex Leicester)
owned by Bill Gates, Seattle, Washington (USA);

Codex Trivulziano in the Biblioteca Trivulziana
in Castello Sforzesco, Milan;

Codex on the Flight of Birds
in the Biblioteca Reale, Turin.

The chronology of Leonardo's notes and drawings
varies frequently even within a single manuscript.
Accordingly, for each image reproduced,
the certain or approximate date is indicated.
Unless otherwise specified, the works reproduced
in this volume are by Leonardo da Vinci.
Where no location is indicated,
the work forms part of a private collection.

Contents

1452/1468 Birth certificate

THE EARLY YEARS

It was the night of April 15, 1452. At Vinci, a country town between Florence and Pistoia, surrounded by the green Tuscan hills, a woman was about to give birth. Her name was Caterina and she was not married. The father of the baby was Ser Piero da Vinci, twenty-five years old, a notary by profession, following the tradition of his family, one of the town's oldest and most prominent, notaries for generations and property owners in the town and its vicinity. As time was then calculated, with the hours of the night starting from sunset, it was the third hour of a Saturday – three hours after 7 in the evening – when Caterina gave birth to her son Leonardo in a house located in the village of Anchiano. It was thus 10 o'clock at night as time is now calculated. The event was punctually recorded by the infant's paternal grandfather, Ser Antonio da Vinci: 'A grandson was born to me, the son of my son Ser Piero, on the day of April 15, a Saturday, at the third hour of the night. He was named Lionardo. He was baptized by the Priest Piero di Bartolomeo da Vinci, Papino di Nanni Banti, Meo di Tonino, Piero di Malvolto, Nanni di Venzo, Arigho di Giovanni Tedescho, Monna Lisa di Domenicho di Brettone, Monna Antonia di Giuliano, Monna Niccholosa del Barna, Mon[n]a Maria, the daughter of Nanni di Venzo, Monna Pippa di Previchone'.

The surprising number of five godfathers and five godmothers of a certain rank at Leonardo's baptism indicates that the birth of an illegitimate son must not have been a problem in

House
of Leonardo da Vinci
at Anchiano
(locality of Vinci,
Florence).

those days, considering that even the Pope – Cesare and Lucrezia Borgia were the children of Alexander VI – had natural sons and daughters without even trying to keep it a secret. The child Leonardo was calmly acknowledged by Ser Piero and went to live with his father in the family home, where he spent his childhood and adolescence; without however, the "happy end" of a marriage between his parents. This was probably because Caterina was a woman from a lower social class, perhaps a servant in the da Vinci home. She was thus sent away, but without tears, considering that she soon married Antonio di Piero

Buti del Vacca, by whom she had another five children; to the satisfaction of all, it might be said, considering that the furnace of the Monastery of San Pier Martire where Caterina's husband worked was managed by Leonardo's father and his uncle Francesco. Ser Piero too, a few months after the birth of his first son, decided to establish a respectable family, taking to wife a sixteen-year-old girl who came from a wealthy Florentine family, Albiera degli Amadori. But the young wife died in childbirth in 1464. Ser Piero then remarried Francesca di Ser Giuliano Lanfredini, but his second wife was childless and died in 1473. Six

Giorgio Vasari,
Portrait of Leonardo,
from **The Lives**,
1568 edition.

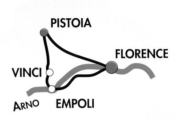

View of Vinci (Florence),
birthplace of Leonardo.

children were instead born of his next marriage, to Margherita di Francesco di Jacopo, and another seven of his last marriage, celebrated in 1485, with Lucrezia di Guglielmo Cortigiani. Leonardo thus had thirteen half-brothers and sisters and several stepmothers with whom he seems to have been on good terms, as indicated by the greeting 'my dear beloved mother' with which, when over fifty, the artist addressed his father's last wife. However, Leonardo almost never mentions in his writings the period spent at Vinci nor his family, and there exists no documentary evidence on the details of his life and early education before he entered the workshop of Verrocchio in Florence, the city to which the adolescent genius moved with his family in 1468.

One hint is however provided by Leonardo himself, who complained in his writings of being a 'man without letters', one without an adequate knowledge of Greek and Latin, deemed indispensable at the time for entering the world of official culture.

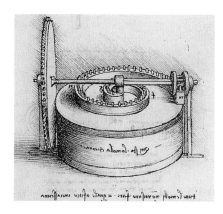

Design for a machine, Codex Madrid I (f. 4r).

Model of revolving crane from a project by Leonardo (1987), Florence, Museo Galileo.

Leonardo tried to remedy this shortcoming in his education after having reached the age of adulthood. In any case, he himself was among the first to proclaim the supremacy of experience over theory, of practical culture over book-learning, rejecting auctoritas, the principle of authority linked to the great names of classical culture. Leonardo was always to show a vein of contention against academic teaching along with the pride of the self-taught, self-made man. It may be that this attitude was rooted in the years of his youth at Vinci, in that country town where as a boy he lived in close contact with nature and the peasant world, where his own family owned farms, a mill (belonging to his uncle Francesco) and a furnace (to his father, Ser Piero). The latter was the ideal place to approach the art

The Museo Leonardiano
in Castello Guidi,
Vinci (Florence).
In the foreground,
the sculpture
by Mario Ceroli,
The Man of Vinci
(1987).

of ceramics, which there are reasons to suppose may have been another of this eclectic artist's fields of interest. But the years in Vinci did not educate Leonardo merely to love of nature and careful observation of it, nor to a just consideration of the role of experience and experimentation viewed as the concrete realization of an idea.

In fact, what might at a first glance seem an insolated country town, devoid of any cultural stimulus, was probably already at the time in vivacious contact with the world. And cities such as Florence, Empoli, Pisa and Pistoia were not so far away even then, as shown by the fact that Leonardo's father went frequently to Florence for his work and that prominent Florentine families and institutions had business interests in Vinci. Moreover, the town was not located in some anonymous area, nor was the

age in which Leonardo lived an anonymous one. It was in fact the Tuscany of the 15th century, the most culturally advanced land of the times, with Florence standing supreme as the center of the known world, the cradle of that ferment of ideals and new achievements that would go down in history as the Italian Renaissance. And the echo of this new phenomenon certainly reached as far as Vinci, influencing local trends in art, as demonstrated by the sculpture of the Magdalene in the Church of Santa Croce, clearly influenced by Donatello. But as previously mentioned, little or nothing is known of Leonardo's early years in his home town. Nor are the artist's old biographies, not always reliable, of any greater help. The first is that of the so-called Anonimo Gaddiano, the unknown Florentine who wrote several biographies of sculptors and

Below:
a room in the Museo
Leonardiano,
Vinci (Florence).

Model of Leonardo's
"automobile"
at the Museo Leonardiano,
Vinci (Florence).

painters around 1540, only slightly over twenty years after the death of Leonardo in 1519. Then there is *The Lives of the most excellent architects, painters and sculptors in Italy from Cimabue up to our own times* by Giorgio Vasari, whose first edition was published in 1550. In the *Life of Leonardo*, which draws on the Anonimo Gaddiano, Vasari rather vaguely mentions the artist's early education at Vinci: 'Truly wondrous and divine was Leonardo, the son of Ser Piero da Vinci; and he would have made great progress in his early studies of literature if he had not been so unpredictable and unstable. For he set about learning many things and, once begun, he would then abandon them. For instance, in the few months he applied himself to arithmetic, Leonardo made such progress that he raised continuous doubts and difficulties for the master who taught him and often confounded him. He turned to music for a while, and soon he decided to learn to play the lyre, like one to whom nature had given a naturally elevated and

**Landscape
with the view
of the Arno**
(1473),
Florence,
Gabinetto Disegni
e Stampe degli Uffizi
(Inv. No. 8 Pr).

refined spirit, and accompanying himself on this instrument, he sang divinely, improvising. But in spite of the fact that he was interested in so many different things, he never gave up drawing and working in relief, activities which appealed to him more than any others'.
Did Leonardo already know how to draw when (as we will see) he entered Verrocchio's workshop in Florence? And if so, had he learned by himself or under a master? To these questions no answer has yet been found. And the mist that obscures the dawn of his first years of apprenticeship thickens due to the lack of works attributed to him before 1473, the date of the drawing of a landscape now in the Uffizi in Florence, which was thus executed at a time when Leonardo had already been apprenticed to the Florentine master for some years, and which remains up to this moment the first known work by his hand.

The walls of Castello Guidi
at Vinci with Ceroli's sculpture
on the bastions.

Seal of the Town of Vinci
(14th century),
Florence, Bargello
National Museum.

AT VINCI SEEKING
THE TRACES OF LEONARDO

No known work by Leonardo remains today in the town where
he was born. Vinci has attempted to fill this gap by dedicating
to its most famous citizen an important museum that celebrates
and documents, amply and clearly, the figure of Leonardo
the inventor, technician and engineer. Founded in 1953
(the fifth centennial of the artist's birth), housed in the medieval
castle of the Guidi Counts, since 2004 the Museo Leonardiano
has expanded to incorporate Palazzina degli Uzielli, facing
on the scenographic square laid out in 2006 by Mimmo Paladino.
The museum displays a vast collection of models of Leonardo's
machines, built on the basis of drawings found in his autograph
codices. A first group of models donated by IBM has been
enriched by new pieces added continuously over the years,
including those of the important travelling exhibition *Laboratorio
Leonardo* (1983-1986), also sponsored by IBM, while others
continue to arrive in a constant process of updating and
investment. In the square before the castle a great wooden
sculpture entitled *L'uomo di Vinci* (*The Man of Vinci*), created
by Mario Ceroli in 1987, materially represents another famous
Leonardian study: the so-called *Homo Vitruvianus*, taken as the
symbolic image of Leonardo's eclectic genius.
Another sculpture bearing homage to Leonardo's genius
is the one in Piazza della Libertà, beside the bronze horse
created in 1997 by Nina Akamu, appearing as the embodiment
of Leonardo's project for the equestrian monument to Francesco
Sforza, Duke of Milan. In addition to the fundamentally important
Museo Leonardiano and the aforesaid sculptures, other institutions
representa true itinerary in honor of this illustrious citizen of Vinci.
First among them, the Biblioteca Leonardiana, a complete, up-to-
date center of documentation and research on the complex figure
of this Renaissance artist. Opened to the public in 1928, although

already established in the late 19th century, it offers a thorough overview of Leonardo's manuscripts, conserved here in facsimile, and the publications dedicated to the personality and the thought of this supreme artist and his times published all over the world.

In 1993 was inaugurated the Museo Ideale Leonardo da Vinci di Arte, Utopia e Cultura della Terra. In addition to documents and testimony of various kinds, linked to the history of Vinci and its territory, there is a vast assortment of material coming from exhibitions held on Leonardo in Italy and abroad, as well as extensive documentation on the fortunes of this personage and his production over the course of time, with the "homage" and "revocations" of many artists, including contemporary ones. Lastly at about 3 km from the town, in the locality of Anchiano, stands the building indicated by tradition as the birthplace of Leonardo.

Open to visitors since 1952, the structure was "rearranged" in 1986. Although none of the original furnishings have remained, the surrounding landscape has lost none of the gentle beauty that must have met the eyes of Leonardo in his time. For this reason, reproductions of views of the Tuscan countryside and a map of the Valdarno drawn by the great artist are displayed.

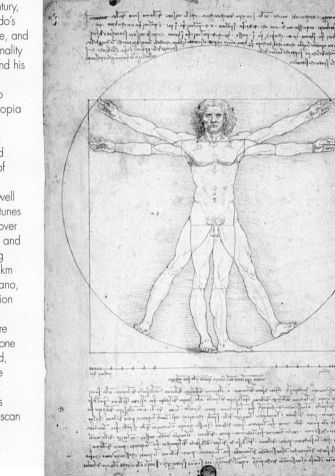

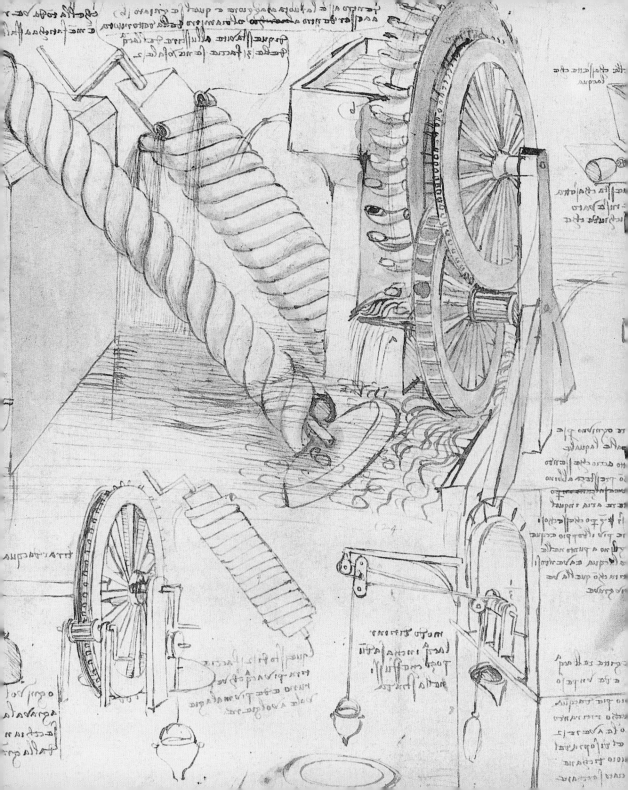

The codices

THE HISTORY OF A DISPERSION

At the death of Leonardo, in 1519, all of his manuscripts – the 'infinity of volumes' seen by Antonio de Beatis in 1517 – were inherited by Francesco Melzi. From Amboise this disciple brought them back to Italy, to his villa at Vaprio d'Adda, where he kept them until 1570. With his son Orazio, uninterested in his father's legacy, began the history of the dispersion of the Leonardian codices – today reduced to one-fifth of the original material – with thefts, disappearance and unexpected discoveries. The first theft of thirteen manuscripts, stolen by a man "above suspicion" in the Melzi home, Gavardi d'Asola, took place in 1585. Three years later there was an "undue appropriation" by canon Ambrogio Mazenta and his brother Guido. Then when seven of the manuscripts taken by the Mazenta brothers were returned to Orazio Melzi, he sold them to Pompeo Leoni, a passionate admirer of Leonardo and the court sculptor at Madrid, where the codices were transferred in 1590. Some of the codices, among them the Codex Atlanticus, returned to Italy, purchased by Count Galeazzo Arconati who in 1637 donated them to the Biblioteca Ambrosiana in Milan. Others ended up in England, where they were brought by Lord Arundel. In 1795 Napoleon took the manuscripts from the Ambrosiana in Milan to Paris. In the mid-19th century the story took another turn with the "case of Guglielmo Libri", a high official in the French Library system who managed to remove several folios from the Leonardian codices kept in Paris and sell them to Lord Ashburnham in England. The Codex Hammer, which

CHRONOLOGICAL TABLE

*Codex Arundel:	1478-1518	Forster II:	1495 and 1497 c.
*Windsor Collection:	1478-1518	(the second and the first part, respectively)	
*Codex Atlanticus:	1478-1518	Manuscript M:	1495-1500
Manuscript B:	1487-1489	Manuscript I:	1497 and 1499
Codex Trivulziano:	1487-1490	(the second and the first part, respectively)	
Forster I:	1487-1490 and 1505	Manuscript L:	1497-1502 and 1504
(the second and the first part, respectively)		Manuscript K:	1503-1505
Manuscript C:	1490-1491	and	1506-1507
Manuscript A:	1490-1492	(the second and the first part, respectively)	
Madrid I, 8937:	1490-1499 and 1508	Codex on the Flight of Bird:	1505
Madrid II, 8936:	1491-1493	Codex Hammer:	1506-1508 and 1510
and	1503-1505	Manuscript F:	1508
(the second and the first part, respectively)		Manuscript D:	1508-1509
Manuscript H:	1493-1494	Manuscript G:	1510-1511 and 1515
Forster III:	1493-1496	Manuscript E:	1513-1514

The oldest folios are found in miscellaneous collections not put together by Leonardo, and which thus cannot be classified among the manuscripts proper. These miscellaneous collections are therefore marked with an asterisk, to indicate that they open the chronology of the material contained in the known Leonardian codices, but not that of the codices proper.

ended up in the United States, was not a part of the Melzi heredity, since its first known owner was, in 1537, the sculptor Guglielmo della Porta. The codex, which belonged to the Count of Leicester in the 18th century, was sold at auction in 1980 and purchased by the American oil millionaire Armand Hammer. Sold again at auction in 1994, the codex is now owned by another famous American entrepreneur Bill Gates.

Original binding of the Codex Atlanticus (16th century), in red leather with gilded decorations, 65 x 44 cm; Milan, Biblioteca Ambrosiana.

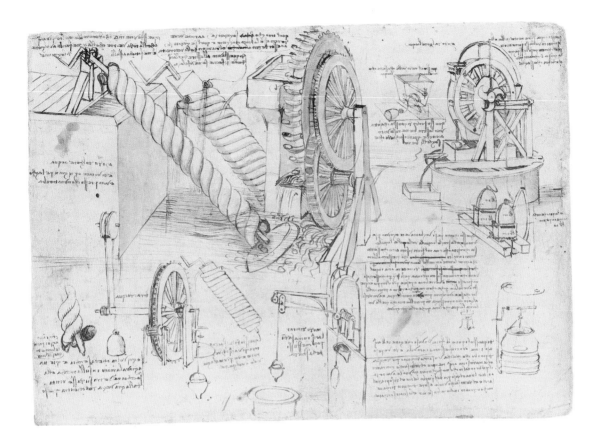

Archimedes' screws
and pumps to raise water
(c. 1480-1482),
Codex Atlanticus (f. 26v).

ITALY

Codex Atlanticus

Milan, Biblioteca Ambrosiana
401 folios (65 x 44 cm); rebound after restoration in 12 volumes with a total of 1.119 folios.
This is a miscellaneous collection of Leonardian material put together by Pompeo Leoni. The sculptor and collector glued together 1.750 folios and scattered fragments on sheets of large format, which were then bound in volumes. The name of the codex derives from the large pages of which it is composed, like those of an atlas. From the chronological viewpoint, its content encompasses a vast span of time, from the master's youth to the end of his life, from 1478 to 1518, and the subjects dealt with differ greatly.

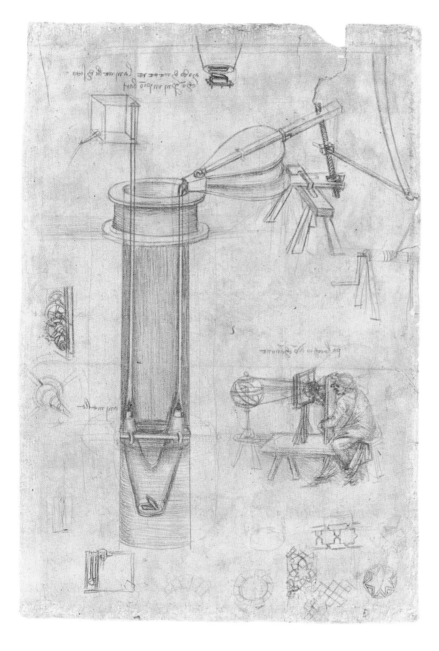

Bellows-operated machine
to raise water and man
with perspectograph
(c. 1480-1482),
Codex Atlanticus (f. 5r).

Draped figure of a man (drunken man?) (c. 1487-1490), Codex Trivulziano (f. 28r).

Codex Trivulziano

Milan, Biblioteca Castello Sforzesco
51 folios (originally 62), c. 20.5 x 14 cm. Included in the donation made by Arconati to the Ambrosiana in 1637, this codex may have been taken back by the Count in exchange for today's Manuscript D, which was later transferred to France with the others from the Milanese library. All trace of it was then lost until it turned up in the possession of Gaetano Caccia, who gave it to Prince Trivulzio in 1750. Dated 1487-1490, it contains lists of Latinisms, caricatures and studies of military and religious architecture.

Codex on the Flight of Birds

Turin, Biblioteca Reale
18 folios, 21 x 15 cm. This little codex was "sewn" inside Manuscript B. In this way it was transferred from the Ambrosiana to the Institut de France. Here it was stolen by Guglielmo Libri, who dismembered it, selling five of the folios in England, while the rest was purchased in the late 19th century by Count Giacomo Manzoni and then by the Russian Prince Theodore Sabachnikoff, who donated it to the Savoia family. Now integral again, the little volume, in which appears the date 1505, contains observations on the behavior of birds in flight and related studies for a flying machine.

Manuscript K,
Paris, Institut de France.

Manuscript I,
Paris, Institut de France.

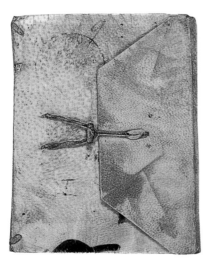

FRANCE

Manuscripts in France
Paris, Institut de France
In the Institut de France are kept all of the manuscripts once in the Milan Biblioteca Ambrosiana – except the Codex Atlanticus, which returned to Italy in 1815 – which were taken by Napoleon to the French library in 1795. According to the late 18th century system, the codices are marked with the letters of the alphabet from A to M. They are volumes of small format, interesting insofar as they faithfully conserve the method followed by Leonardo in compiling them. In addition to the characteristic reverse writing, from right to left, deriving from the fact that the master was left-handed, can be observed his habit of proceeding from the back of the book toward the beginning, and his practice of making notes, turning the sheets upside-down when necessary. Two categories of codices appear in this group: the first includes volumes written in more orderly manner, usually by pen, which were probably compiled in the studio; the second consists of smaller booklets, hastily written, often in red pencil, which were probably utilized in precarious situations, outdoors for instance.

Fruit and vegetables,
architectural layouts,
groups of
non-deciphered letters
(c. 1487-1489),
Manuscript B
(f. 23r), detail.

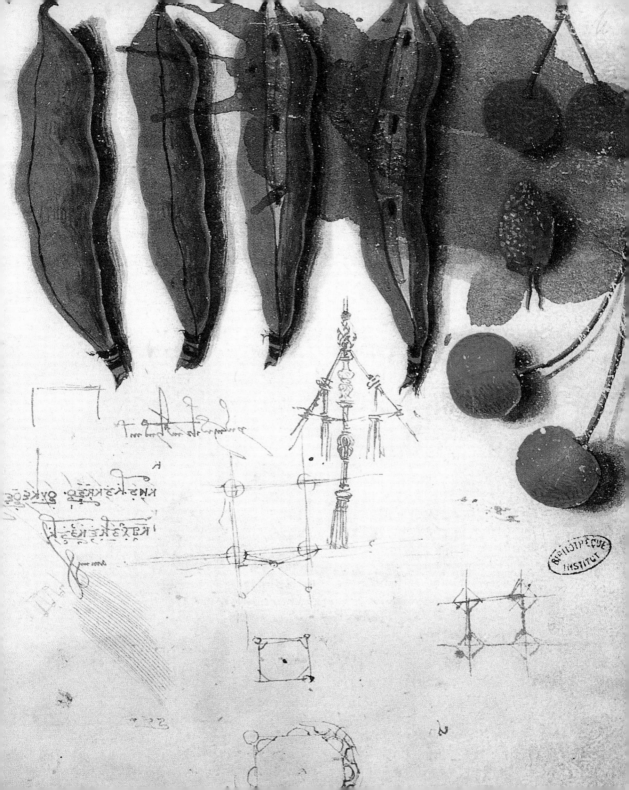

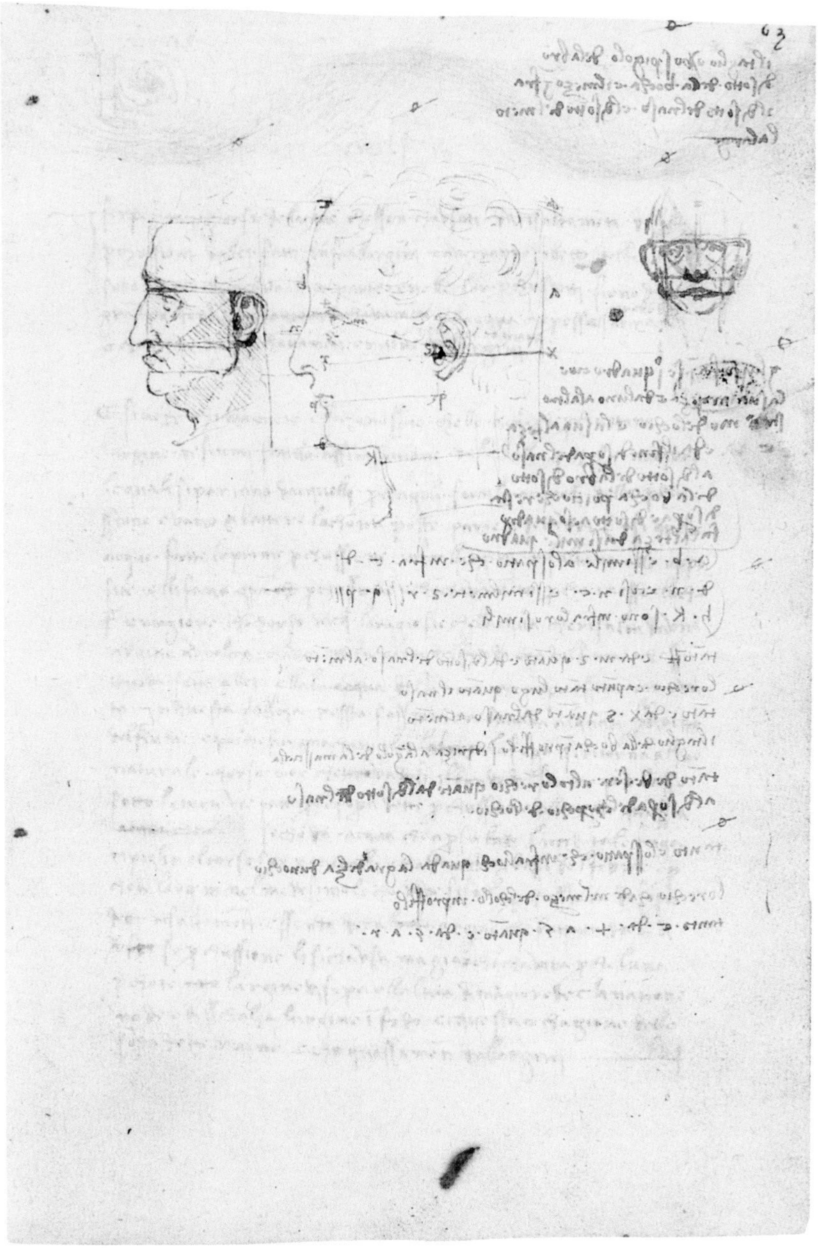

Studies of human head (c. 1490-1492), Manuscript A (f. 63r).

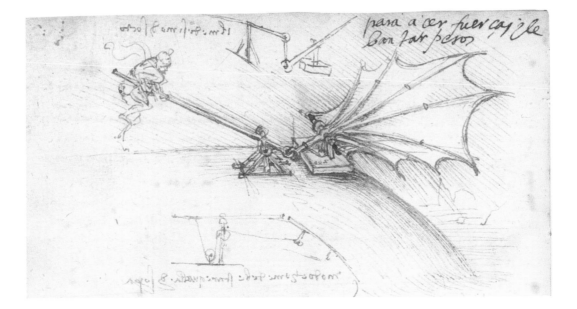

Study to test the force required to move the wing in the flying machine (c. 1487-1490), Manuscript B (f. 88v), detail.

Manuscript A

63 folios (originally 114), 22 x 15 cm. The original manuscript has been mutilated by the theft of numerous folios – some never found again – removed in the mid-19th century by Guglielmo Libri, who put some of the sheets together again in a volume which he sold to the English Lord Ashburnham. This volume was then retrieved and cataloged as Ashburnham 2038. The manuscript, dated 1490-1492, is predominantly concerned with painting and physics, with remarks on motion serving as common denominator. The theme of painting is discussed in detail, so much so that Francesco Melzi transcribed ample parts of it in his *Libro di pittura* – later published in the mid-17th century as *Trattato della pittura* – in which Leonardo's pupil collected his master's observations on the subject.

Manuscript B

84 folios (originally 100), c. 23 x 16 cm. This manuscript is mutilated like the previous one, a number of folios having been stolen by Guglielmo Libri and then put together in a volume and sold to Lord Ashburnham. After their retrieval, the part that had been removed was cataloged

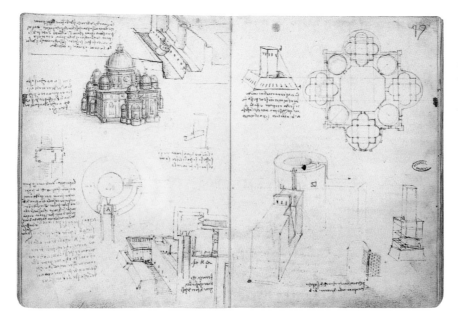

Church with circular plan
seen in "birds-eye view"
and layout,
along with drawings
of military architecture
(c. 1487-1490),
Manuscript B
(ff. 18v and 19r).

under the indication Ashburnham 2037. Compiled between 1487 and 1490, this manuscript is, along with the Codex Trivulziano, the oldest of Leonardo's codices. The master began to record his thought in writing rather late when, by now thirty-five years old, he finally managed to overcome his youthful distaste for letters. Drawings of weapons and military or industrial machines, circular churches, the famous "ideal city" on two levels and above all the futuristic projects for flying machines and other inventions – from an aerial screw that seems to anticipate the helicopter to a submarine – make up the body of material in this codex.

Manuscript C
32 folios, 31.5 x 22 cm.

This was one of the manuscripts remaining with the Mazenta brothers after the theft of Gavardi d'Asola in the Melzi home, and was thus not among the codices in the Leoni heredity purchased by Arconati and then sold to the Biblioteca Ambrosiana. It was instead donated to the Milan library in 1609 by its founder, Cardinal Federigo Borromeo, to whom it had been given by Guido Mazenta. It may have contained another notebook, now lost. The codex bears the date on which it was begun, April 23, 1490, and it was probably finished

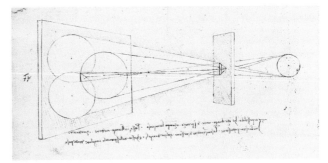

Eye and rays of light
(c. 1508-1509),
Manuscript D
(f. 1v), detail.

Rays of light through
an angular opening
(c. 1490-1491),
Manuscript C (f. 10v).

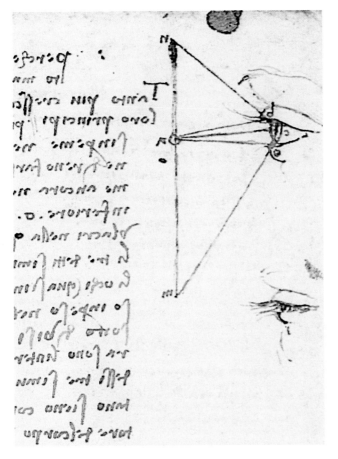

within 1491. Its content deals mainly with the effects of light and shadow on different shapes and surfaces.

Manuscript D

10 folios, 22.5 x 16 cm.

It may have been exchanged, in the donation made by Arconati, for the Codex Trivulziano, taken back by the Count. Dated 1508-1509, it contains mainly studies on the structure of the eye and the nature of vision, conducted through comparison with the hypotheses of ancient authors, and through experience, with the dissection of cadavers, glass models of the eye and the preparation of a camera oscura.

Manuscript E

80 folios (originally 96), 14.5 x 10 cm. Mutilated by the removal of a group of folios stolen by Guglielmo Libri and then lost. This is a late codex, dating from 1513-1514. It focuses predominantly on two subjects: mechanical physics

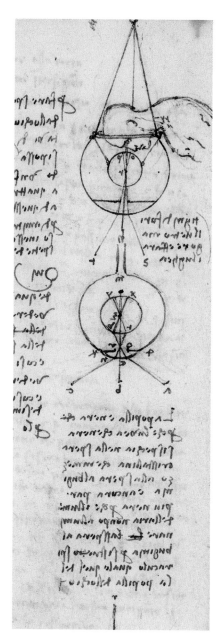

and the flight of birds, linked to the invention of a flying machine, whose design has evolved from that of a device operated by beating wings to a kind of glider exploiting currents of air.

Manuscript F

96 folios, 14.5 x 10 cm.
The manuscript has survived intact from when it was compiled, in very brief time, in 1508. The main theme is the study of water, with examples of rare graphic mastery in drawing the complicated forms in which the liquid element can appear. An important section of the manuscript is dedicated to optics and the study of light, from which the discussion goes on to cosmology, with the hypothesis that the Earth may have originated by emerging from the waters of the sea.

Manuscript G

93 folios, 14.5 x 10 cm (with perhaps three sheets removed originally).
The dates appearing in the codex (1510, 1511 and 1515) refer, the first two, to the second Milanese period, the third to Leonardo's stay in Rome. Among the many subjects dealt with, botany is particularly important.

Manuscript H

142 folios, 10.5 x 8 cm.
This is composed of three different notebooks, which may have been bound

Observer looking into a glass model of the human eye (c. 1508-1509), Manuscript D (f. 3v), detail.

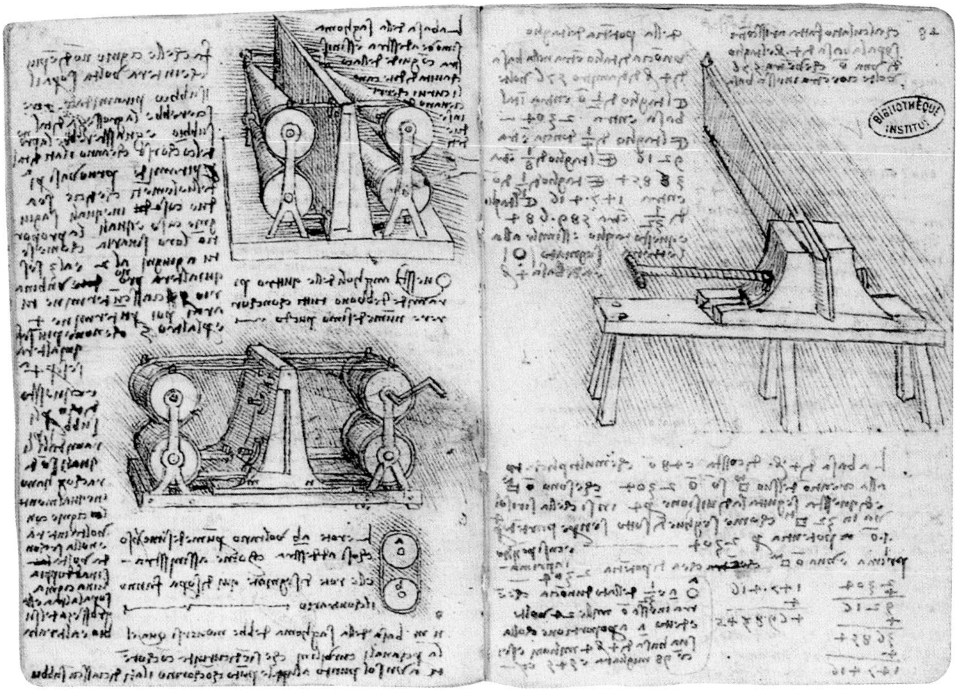

Machinery
for manufacturing
concave mirrors, study
on shearing power with
mathematical calculations
(c. 1515),
Manuscript G
(ff. 83v and 84r).

together after the death of Pompeo Leoni. It is dedicated to the study of water. Interesting notes on Latin grammar show that Leonardo, now over forty, had resumed studying this subject. The codex dates from 1493-1494, dates referred to in all three notebooks.

Manuscript I

I^1 48 folios and I^2 91 folios, 10 x 7.5 cm. The manuscript is formed of two notebooks which differ as concerns number of folios and which proceed in reverse chronological order, the first one being

dated 1499 and the second 1497. They deal with various subjects: one of the curiosities is the measurement of Leonardo's vineyard at San Vittore.

Manuscript K

K^1 48 folios, K^2 32 folios, K^3 48 folios, 9.6 x 6.5 cm.
Although included in the Leoni heredity, the manuscript did not enter the Biblioteca Ambrosiana through the Arconati donation, but was sold to it in 1674 by Count Orazio Archinti. It is composed of three notebooks, the first

two dating from 1503-1505 and the last from 1506-1507. The dominant theme, especially in the first two notebooks, is geometry, with the interesting problem of squaring the circle.

Manuscript L

94 folios (originally 96), 10 x 7 cm. This manuscript has retained the characteristics it possessed at the time it was compiled, in the years 1497 to 1502 with additions up to 1504. The notes on the Last Supper are one of the most interesting elements in this codex. But equally important and quite extensive are the sections dedicated to the military fortifications designed by the master while he was in the service of Cesare Borgia, and those on the flight of birds, with various designs for a flying machine. Among the curiosities is a sketch of the gigantic bridge designed to connect 'Pera and Gostantinopoli', of which Leonardo wrote in a letter to the Turkish sultan.

Manuscript M

96 folios, c. 10 x 7 cm. Compiled starting from 1495, it contains studies and reflections from 1499-1500, when Leonardo committed himself to a fundamental confrontation with some of the great thinkers of antiquity, such as Euclid and Aristotle. Much space is dedicated, in this codex, to geometry and physics.

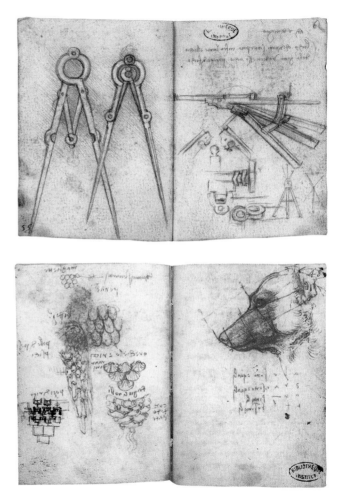

Two types of adjustable-opening compass, mortar-piece and mechanical parts (c. 1493-1494), Manuscript H (ff. 108v and 109r).

Studies of decorative motifs and proportions of the head of a dog (c. 1497-1498), Manuscript I (ff. 47v and 48r).

LEONARDIAN INSTITUTIONS THROUGHOUT THE WORLD

The network of international institutions and research organizations which has grown up around the complex figure of Leonardo began with some specialized libraries, the oldest of which is the Biblioteca Leonardiana at Vinci, founded in 1898, followed by the Raccolta Vinciana in Milan (publisher of the year-book of the same name) founded in 1905, and the Elmer Belt Library of Vinciana in Los Angeles, donated by the founder to the University of California in 1961. Here Armand Hammer, for whom the Codex Hammer (now Leicester) was named, sponsors a Chair of Vincian Studies and a Center of Vincian Studies, both directed by Carlo Pedretti. In Los Angeles, Carlo Pedretti has also established an important foundation, with a European base in his villa at Castel Vitoni in Lamporecchio, above Vinci.
In addition to these are numerous other institutions and initiatives concerning Leonardo. Thye include the Museo Ideale of Vinci directed by Alessandro Vezzosi and the publication in facsimile of all of the Leonardian codices undertaken, with the contribution of the Fondazione Leonardo da Vinci of Florence, by the Giunti publishing house.

From above:
Bulletin of the Centro
Ricerche Leonardiane
of Brescia.

The Year-Book
of the Hammer Center,
Los Angeles.

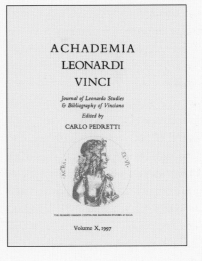

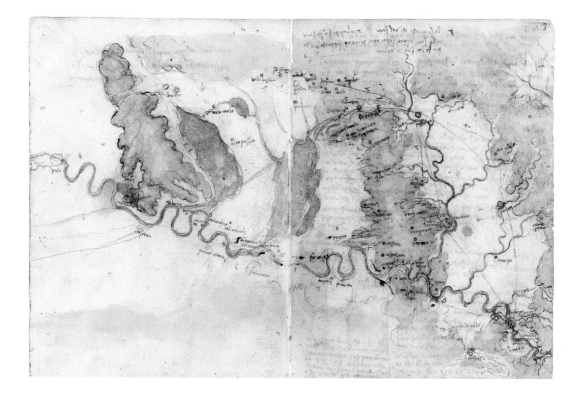

SPAIN

Madrid Manuscripts

Madrid, Biblioteca Nacional
These are two manuscripts found by chance in the Spanish library only in 1966. For centuries their existence was unknown, due to the erroneous indications under which they had been catalogued upon entering the Biblioteca Reale in 1830, where they were inventoried for the first time in 1831-1833. The two codices belonged to Don Juan Espina, who probably acquired them through the Leoni heredity, and they are almost certainly the ones that Lord Arundel tried to buy in the 1630s, and those to which Vincente Carducho referred in 1633, stating that Espina intended to donate them to the King of Spain, which seems to be what actually happened at the death of the Spanish gentleman.

Map of Tuscany
with course of the Arno
River from Florence
down to Pisa and the sea
(c. 1504),
Codex Madrid II
(ff. 22v and 23r).

Madrid I, 8937

184 folios (8 missing, perhaps from the time of Leonardo), 21 x 15 cm. These folios were compiled during the years 1490 to 1499, with additions up to 1508. Drawings of mechanisms of various types, including clocks, fill the first part of the codex, while the second is dedicated to studies of theoretical mechanics.

Madrid II, 8936

157 folios, 21 x 15 cm. The codex is formed of two manuscripts totally different in content and chronology. The first dates from 1503-1505, while the second (ff. 141-157) is clearly datable to the Milan years between 1491 and 1493. The volume is important for a knowledge of some aspects of Leonardo's activity. Extremely interesting drawings are those concerning the project for deviating the Arno during the war between Florence and Pisa, while some contemporaneous notes provide precious information on the Battle of Anghiari. Other observations concern perspective and optics, and were utilized by Melzi for his *Libro di Pittura*. The last part of the codex is dedicated to the casting of the Sforza Monument.

Clockwork spring and device for automatic release of loads; set of linked chains (c. 1495-1499), Codex Madrid I (ff. 9v and 10r).

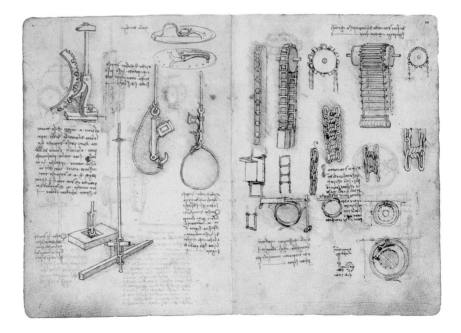

ENGLAND

Windsor Collection

Windsor Castle, Royal Library
234 folios.

A miscellaneous collection put together not by Leonardo but by Pompeo Leoni, as in the case of the Codex Atlanticus. In 1630 the codex was in the possession of Thomas Howard, Count of Arundel, who had bought it in Spain from the sculptor's heirs. How it then entered the collections of the English Crown is still a mystery. It is known that Lord Arundel left England in 1645, during the civil war, to settle in Amsterdam, where he brought his collection of drawings. But it is not known whether the Leonardian volume passed to Windsor from Holland, or whether it had already arrived there previously. In the first case it may be hypothesized that the codex had entered into the possession of the court painter Sir Peter Lely, who may have sold or donated it to King Charles II. In any case, by 1690 it already formed part of the royal collections, as proven by the fact that it was shown in that year to Constantijn Huygens, secretary to William III and himself a collector. The codex contains nearly six hundred drawings by Leonardo dating from the period 1478 to 1518. Today, after a long operation beginning in the late 19th century, the individual folios with Leonardo's drawings have each been placed between

Study of muscles
of the trunk and thigh
(c. 1510),
Windsor (RL 19014v),
whole and detail.

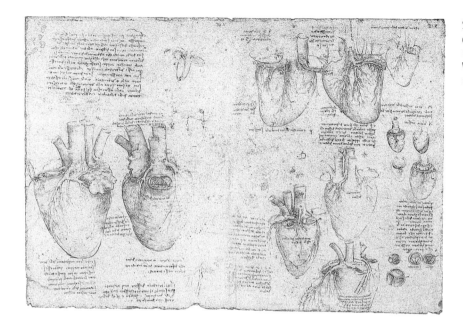

Superficial veins
of the heart
(c. 1513),
Windsor
(RL 19073v-19074v).

two sheets of perspex and divided into
thematic sections: anatomy – landscapes
– horses and other animals – figures, pro-
files, caricatures – miscellaneous papers.

Codex Arundel

London, British Library
283 folios, mainly 21 x 15 cm.
This too is a miscellaneous collection not
put together by Leonardo. However, unlike the Codex Atlanticus and the Windsor Collection, it is not an assemblage
of folios and fragments but a group of
booklets which have more or less retained their original structure, although a
few individual folios with different dates

have been inserted in some of the notebooks. This codex was not one of those
in the Pompeo Leoni heredity, but was
almost certainly bought by Lord Arundel, alias Thomas Howard, in Spain in
the 1630s. In any case, it was certainly in the library of his English home in
1642, and passed down to his heirs
after his death, which took place in Italy
in 1646. Here the great art collector,
ceaselessly on the hunt for Leonardian
material, journeyed often and had also
contacted Count Arconati in the unsuccessful attempt to purchase from him the
Codex Atlanticus. In 1666 the Codex
Arundel was donated by its new owners

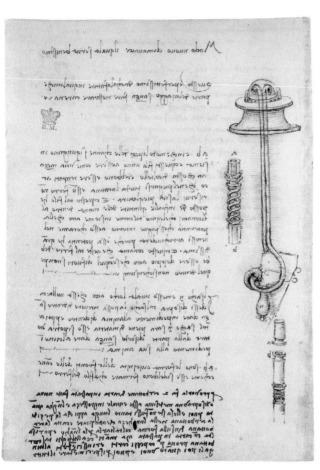

Study of floater
with breathing tubes
for diver (c. 1508),
Codex Arundel (f. 24v).

to the Royal Society of London, and from there it arrived at the British Museum in 1831-1832. As regards chronology, the span of time encompassed by this codex is vast, ranging from 1478 to 1518. Its main subject is mathematics, but there is a great variety of content, ranging from physics to optics to architecture. To the latter field belong the drawings for the palace of Romorantin, designed by Leonardo in his last three years of life, during his stay in France. Famous is the note concerning the death of his father, written in a cool, detached tone, almost in the style of a notary's document: 'On the 9th day of July, 1504, a Wednesday, at the hour of 7 o'clock died Ser Piero Davincj, notary at the Palace of the Podestà, my father, at the hour of 7 o'clock. He was 80 years old, he left 10 sons and 2 daughters'. Among the curiosities is the "diver's mask", a futuristic drawing of a device for breathing under water.

Codices Forster

London, Victoria and Albert Museum
These are three codices of small format, similar to pocket notebooks, different in content and dating. They first belonged to Count Lytton, who may perhaps have acquired them through the Leoni heredity, and then to John Forster, who at his death (1876) left them to the London institution.

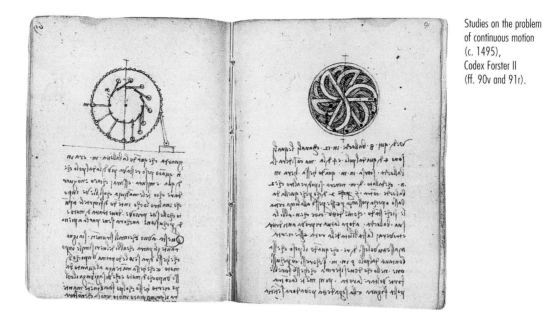

Studies on the problem
of continuous motion
(c. 1495),
Codex Forster II
(ff. 90v and 91r).

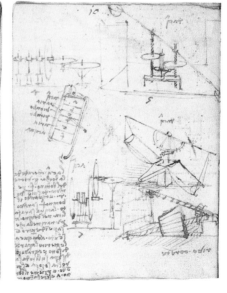

Figure of seated woman
with child in her lap
(c. 1497),
Codex Forster II (f. 37r).

Gears to move
hydraulic pumps
(c. 1487-1490),
Codex Forster I (f. 45v).

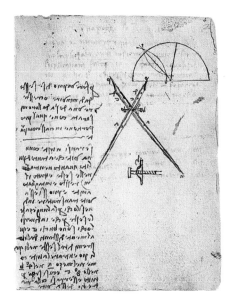

Geometric figure,
proportional compass
and its nut screw
(c. 1505),
Codex Forster I (f. 4r).

Forster I

FI[1] 40 folios and FI[2] 14 folios,
c. 14.5 x 10 cm.
The codex is divided into two manuscripts, the first of which, dated 1505, is later than the second, which dates from 1487-1490. FI[1] appears as a well-structured organic section, with an order rather unusual for Leonardo. The main subject, linked to the interest in geometry that had become fundamentally important through his friendship with Luca Pacioli, is stereometry, i.e., the 'transformation [...] of one body into another without decrease or increase in matter'. FI[2] contains studies from the first Milanese period, especially on hydraulic engineering, with drawings of "Archimedes' screws" to raise water and other hydraulic machines.

Forster II

FII[1] 63 folios and FII[2] 95 folios, 9.5 x 7 cm. Like the previous codex, it consists of two manuscripts, which an erroneous 17th century binding has joined, reversing them in respect to each other. FII[1], with its references to the *Last Supper* and the architectural studies referring to the works of Bramante in Santa Maria delle Grazie, and with mention of the vineyard at San Vittore, seems to date from around 1497. Outstanding among the many beautiful drawings are those of knots

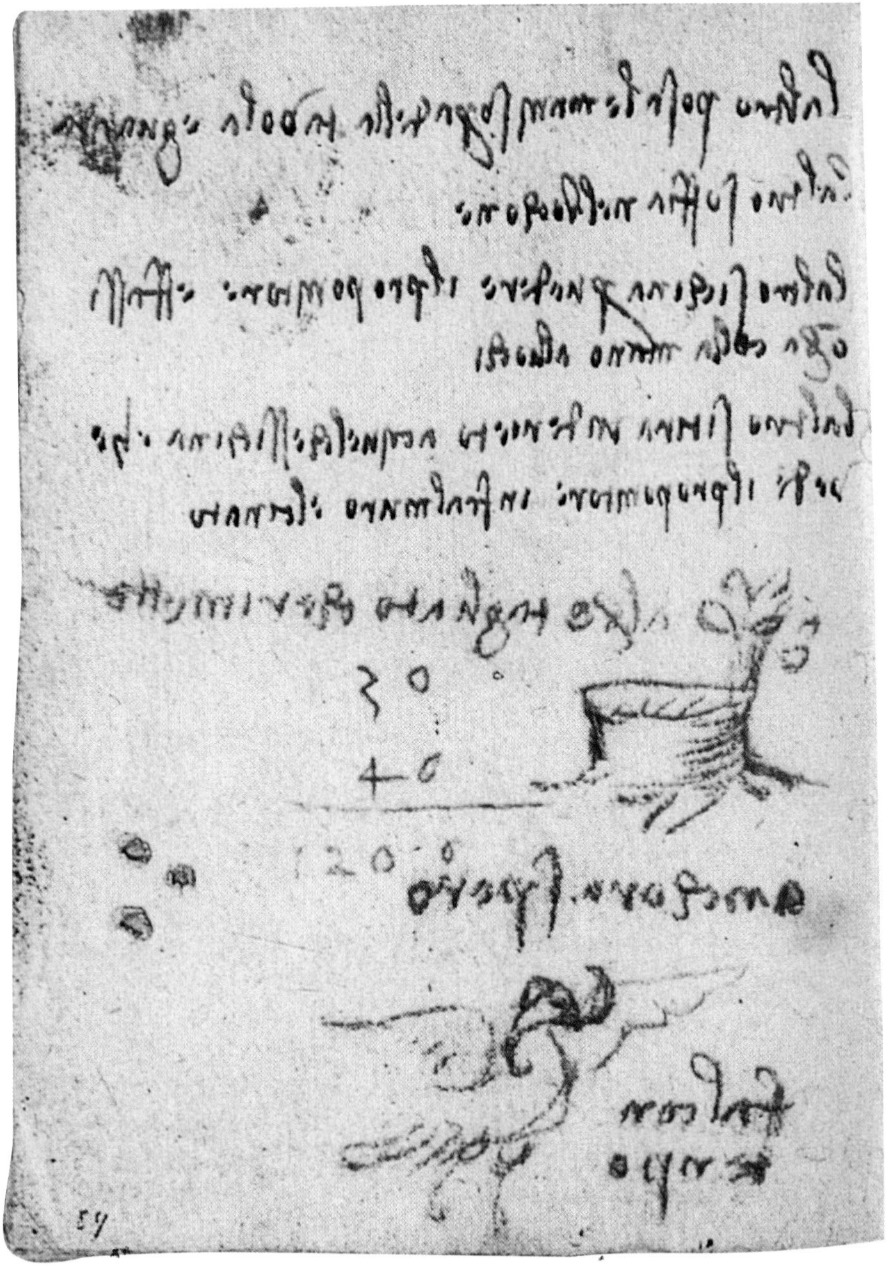

Notes for the
Last Supper
(c. 1495);
emblematic rebus;
falcon holding in its beak
a clock balance-wheel,
Codex Forster II (f. 63r).

Drawings of hats,
ribbons and other articles
of clothing for asquerades
(c. 1494),
Codex Forster III
(ff. 8v and 9r).

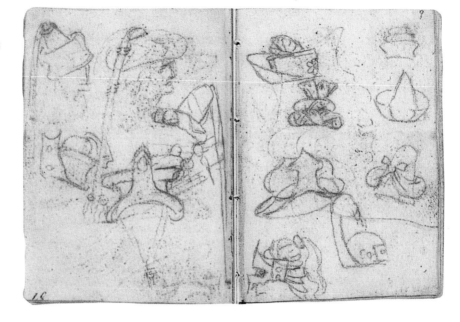

(the so-called 'Vincian knots') and interwoven plants. FII[2] was instead compiled in 1495. It is essentially a notebook of exercises which reflect Leonardo's undying passion for physics, presenting a series of studies linked to the writing of a theoretical treatise on the subject – now lost – mentioned by Leonardo in his notes. Among its curiosities is a note of expenses for the 'burial of Caterina', which may refer to Leonardo's mother.

Forster III

94 folios, 9 x 6 cm.
This little volume, written mostly in red pencil, has the characteristics of a "brogliaccio", with notes and extemporaneous sketches of all types scattered over the pages with no precise order. It contains material referring to the years of Leonardo's wide-ranging activity at the court of Ludovico il Moro, probably collected around 1493-1496.

Among other things it contains fables, recipes, moral pronouncements, masks, hats, as well as drawings for the Sforza Monument and architectural and urban planning studies for the city of Milan.

THE UNITED STATES

Codex Hammer

Seattle, Bill Gates Collection
18 double sheets, i.e. 36 folios with recto and verso, 29 x 22 cm
Leonardo compiled this codex gradually by pen, filling one double folio after another and inserting each one among those previously completed. Perhaps he intended to have the pages sewn together to form a real book. Today, after disassembly of the volume, the folios are loose as when they were compiled.
The codex taked its name from its former owner, the American Armand Hammer, who bought it at auction in 1980. Now it is known as the Codex Leicester too, in this case too from the name of its owner, Thomas Coke Count of Leicester, who bought it from the painter Giuseppe Ghezzi in 1717.
Going still further back, we finally arrive at the first owner of the manuscript, who in 1537 was the Milanese sculptor Guglielmo della Porta, who evidently acquired it since the volume was not inherited by Francesco Melzi. Its latest owner is the American Bill Gates, the computer king, who bought the Codex Hammer in 1994, when it was sold at auction. Leonardo compiled the manuscript

Studies on water and drawings of ramps to slow down water fall (c. 1506-1508), Codex Hammer (f. 22r, detail).

Page of notes on the Moon; drawings and notes on the light of the Sun, the Earth and the Moon (c. 1506-1508), Codex Hammer (ff. 36v and 1r).

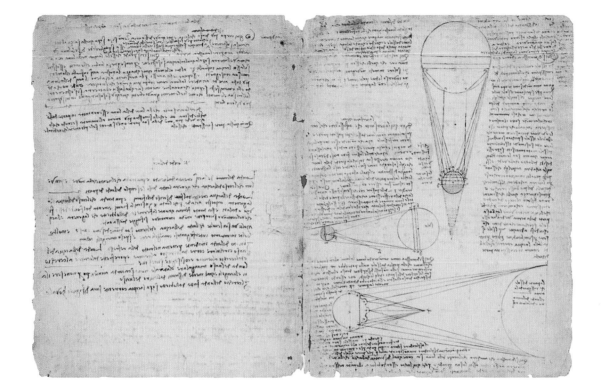

Study on force
and equilibrium
of a swing
(c. 1506-1508),
Codex Hammer
(f. 8r), detail.

during the two years 1506-1508, with additions up to 1510.

His main subject was water, with studies and splendid drawings of currents and whirlpools. Astronomy also plays an important part, with the theme of illumination of the Sun, the Earth and the Moon.

Studies of astronomy
with explanation of the
"earth-shine"
of the new moon
(c. 1508),
Codex Hammer
(ff. 35v and 2r).

Experiments with siphons
of various kinds
for studies
on communicating vessels
(c. 1508)
Codex Hammer
(f. 34v).

1468/1499 Early training and achievements

La Belle Ferronnière
(c. 1495),
detail,
Paris, Musée du Louvre.

A TALENTED APPRENTICE

Leonardo arrived in Florence at the age of sixteen, in 1468. His father, Ser Piero, became the notary of the family in power, the Medici, a position which was undoubtedly advantageous to his son's career. A year later, in 1469, the rule of the most famous Medici of all, Lorenzo the Magnificent, was inaugurated. The first house in which Leonardo is reported to have lived with his father and his young stepmother was in Via de' Gondi, not far from Palazzo della Signoria. Ser Piero moved there in 1469. The building belonged to one of the city's many guilds, that of the

Francesco
and Raffaello Petrini,
**Semi-perspective
view from
Monte Oliveto**
(1887), copy of the
Pianta della catena
attributed to Francesco
di Jacopo Rosselli
(c. 1471-1482; Berlin,
Kupferstichkabinett),
Florence,
Museo Storico-Topografico
"Firenze com'era".

Francesco
and Raffaello Petrini,
**Semi-perspective
view from
Monte Oliveto**
(1887), copy
of the **Pianta
della catena**
attributed to Francesco
di Jacopo Rosselli
(c. 1471-1482; Berlin,
Kupferstichkabinett), detail,
Florence,
Museo Storico-Topografico
"Firenze com'era".

Merchants. Later, starting in 1490, the Gondi family commissioned Giuliano da Sangallo to build its new palace. An idea of how Florence must have looked at the time of Leonardo's first stay in the city is given by the map drawn in 1469 by Pietro del Massaio Fiorentino, and by the map known as *Pianta della catena*, executed around 1472. In the second half of the 15th century the Tuscan capital appears as a flourishing city, active and densely populated, with an urban fabric already rich in splendid public buildings such as Palazzo della Signoria and Palazzo del Bargello, as well as magnificent churches such as San Lorenzo, Santa Croce, Santa Maria Novella, Santa Maria del Carmine, Santo Spirito and the Cathedral of Santa Maria del Fiore,

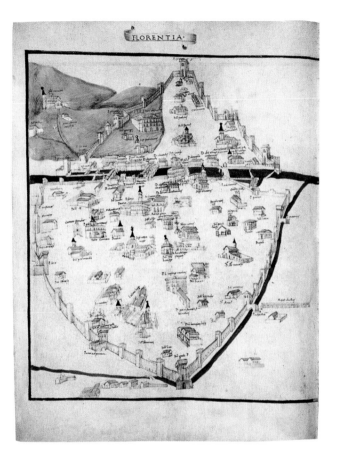

Pietro del Massaio
Fiorentino,
Map of Florence
(1469),
with the main
monuments the city,
Vatican City, Biblioteca
Apostolica Vaticana.

recently completed with the famous dome designed by Brunelleschi. Within this context, the elegant palaces of the great families were rising in rapid succession, stately homes such as the Medici Palace in Via Larga (today's Via Cavour), commissioned by Cosimo de' Medici of Michelozzo in 1444, and the residence designed by Leon Battista Alberti for the Rucellai family, as well as the palace then being built for the fabulously wealthy Luca Pitti.

In the *Rhymed Chronicle* by Giovanni Santi, Raphael's father, who in 1468 was traveling to Milan in the entourage of Federigo da Montefeltro, Leonardo is mentioned among the promising young talents of Florence, one of the cities where the Duke of Urbino stopped along the way: 'Two young

men equal in station and in love / Leonardo da Vinci and the Perusino Pier della Pieve [Perugino] who is a divine painter'. This is confirmation of Leonardo's precocious artistic talent and his inclination for painting; a passion that may have been the real motive – although this is still unproven – that urged the talented adolescent to enter the art workshop of Verrocchio, one of the most famous Florentine masters of the Quattrocento, highly esteemed by prominent clients, among them the Medici family.

The year when Leonardo entered Verrocchio's workshop is usually considered to be 1469. Recording the event in question Vasari, in his *Lives*, reports that it was Ser Piero to take the initiative: 'He took one day some of his [Leonardo's] drawings and brought them to Andrea del Verrocchio, who was a good friend of his, and urgently begged him to say whether Leonardo would profit by studying drawing. Andrea was amazed when he saw Leonardo's extraordinary beginnings, and he urged Ser Piero to have him study this subject; and so Piero arranged for Leonardo to go to Andrea's workshop, which Leonardo was very happy to do. And not this profession alone did he practice, but all those involving drawing. And he had an intellect so divine and marvelous that, being an excellent geometer, not only did he work in sculpture but also in architecture. In his youth he fashioned in clay the heads of some women laughing, created through the craft of plaster casting, as well as the heads of some putti, which seemed to have come from the hand of a master. In architecture he made many drawings of both plans and other buildings, and was again the first who, as a young man, spoke of channeling the Arno River from Pisa to Florence. He drew plans for mills, fulling machines and devices that could be driven by water power; and since painting was to be his profession, he carefully studied this

Study of hands (c. 1475-1480 or 1488-1489), Windsor (RL 12558).

Andrea del Verrocchio's circle, **Bust of Lorenzo the Magnificent** (c. 1492), Washington, National Gallery of Art.

Andrea del Verrocchio, **David** (c. 1465), Florence, Bargello National Museum.

THE ARTIST'S WORKSHOP IN 15th CENTURY FLORENCE

The workshop of Andrea del Verrocchio was a typical example of those to be found in 15th century Florence. The Renaissance workshop was not only the place where artists were trained, but also a profitable business where a certain number of pupils, directed by an affirmed master, worked incessantly to produce complex achievements such as great cycles of frescoes and works of widely varying type. Apprentices usually entered the workshop very early, at about the age of ten. During the first year of apprenticeship they acquired basic technical knowledge. At first an apprentice was assigned almost exclusively to drawing, silver point or drawings in ink on white paper or colored in tempera. The teaching did not focus on theoretical knowledge but on those practical acquirements that, in the shortest possible time, would allow the apprentice to work actively beside his master. The typical workshop did not specialize in any specific branch of art, but made its apprentices experts in a wide range of techniques – drawing, painting, etching, sculpturing, and goldsmithry. In Verrocchio's shop, presumably located around 1470 in his house at the crossroads of Via dell'Agnolo and today's Via de' Macci, Leonardo had companions who were also to become famous, from Botticelli to Perugino, Lorenzo di Credi and Domenico del Ghirlandaio. The latter then opened with his brother Davide another famous shop, where the young Michelangelo worked in 1488.

Angel's head,
study for the **Baptism
of Christ** by Andrea
del Verrocchio and Leonardo
(c. 1475),
Turin, Biblioteca Reale
(Inv. No. 15635).

Andrea del Verrocchio
and Leonardo,
Baptism of Christ
(c. 1473-1478), detail,
Florence, Uffizi Gallery.

art by drawing from life and sometimes by preparing models or clay figures, which he covered with soft rags
dipped in plaster and then patiently
sketched upon very fine Rheims can-
vases or worn linen, working in black
and white with the tip of his brush,
in marvelous manner'. In this passage Vasari clearly emphasizes both
the wealth of experience opened up
to Leonardo when he entered Verroc-

chio's renowned shop, and the great
talent of this "enfant prodige", his genius, which could develop and find its
best expression in this encounter with
the customary broad range of workshop techniques.
In 1476 Leonardo was still working
in Verrocchio's shop. And until 1472
he was enrolled in the Corporation of
San Luca, the association of Florentine painters, and was thus allowed
to receive commissions on his own.
The first work certainly and entirely
by his hand known to us today is the
drawing of a landscape now in the
Uffizi, dated 'the day of Santa Maria
della Neve, the 5th of August 1473'.
Here the twenty-one-year-old artist
depicted the valley of the Arno seen
from above, from the slopes of Mon-
talbano, in the vicinity of Vinci.
At the school of Verrocchio, Leonardo
probably collaborated on some works
which were, however, commissioned
of the Florentine master and paid directly and exclusively to him. These
were not paintings alone – including,
in the opinion of some experts, the
Ruskin Madonna, the *Detroit Adoration* and the *Camaldoli Madonna* –
but also sculptures, the art in which
Verrocchio excelled. In the latter field,
the intervention of the precocious adolescent may even have extended
to such famous works as the *Noble-*

woman with a Bouquet and the David (both now in the Bargello Museum), the slender figure which, it has been suggested, may be a portrait of Leonardo as a youth.

For the angel attributed to Leonardo in the panel depicting the Baptism of Christ (now in the Uffizi), probably painted between 1473 and 1478, originally for the Florentine church of San Salvi, an anecdote related by Vasari states that Verrocchio abandoned the work, forced to admit the superiority of his young apprentice: 'Never again did he wish to work with colors, indignant that a young boy knew more than he'. Again in 1478, another work that Verrocchio, occupied in Venice in designing the monument to the Condottiero Bartolomeo Colleoni, probably entrusted to Leonardo and Lorenzo di Credi to finish, is an important altarpiece for the Pistoia Duomo, the Madonna di Piazza. A part of the predella (now in the Louvre) portraying the Annunciation is attributed to Leonardo.

As for the paintings entirely and indubitably attributable to Leonardo, it should be recalled primarily that they are few in number.

Among the first trials of the superb artist may be listed some works obviously influenced by Verrocchio, such as the Virgin with the Flowers, the Benois Madonna and the lost Madonna with

Andrea del Verrocchio
and Leonardo,
Baptism of Christ
(1473-1478),
Florence, Uffizi Gallery.

**Virgin
with the Flowers**
(c. 1478-1481),
Munich, Bayerische
Staatsgëmaldesammlungen,
Alte Pinakothek.

Andrea del Verrocchio,
**Noblewoman
with a Bouquet**
(c. 1475),
Florence, Bargello
National Museum.

the *Cat*. Uncertainty still remains for the *Dreyfus Madonna* at the National Gallery in Washington, with the critics disagreeing as to whether it should be attributed to Leonardo or to Lorenzo di Credi. Then there is the first and only Florentine portrait, that of *Ginevra Benci*, probably dating from around 1475. As in the other Leonardian portraits, this one too is a half-bust figure reminiscent of the busts sculpted by Verrocchio, in particular the so-called *Noblewoman with a Bouquet* or *Lady of the beautiful hands*. But in Leonardo's painting the view of the figure does not include the detail of the hands, so decisive in Verrocchio's sculpture. However, the incomplete emblem of the Florentine noblewoman on the back of the panel proves that the work has been trimmed at the bottom and that the missing piece must have been large enough to contain the arms and hands arranged as in Verrocchio's sculpture.

Ginevra Benci
(c. 1474-1476), Washington, National Gallery of Art.

THE FLORENCE OF LORENZO THE MAGNIFICENT

Portrait of Lorenzo de' Medici
(c. 1483-1485),
Windsor (RL 12442).

In 1469 Lorenzo de' Medici, became lord of Florence.
He was called the Magnificent for his political and diplomatic
skill and for his activity as generous patron of the arts,
qualities that were to make him the very symbol of Florence
in the 15th century and more generally of the Italian Renaissance.
Born in 1449 to Piero de' Medici and Lucrezia Tornabuoni,
Lorenzo was the grandson of Cosimo the Elder, the founder
of the Medici dynasty. He came to power very young, at the age
of twenty, subsequent to the early death of his father, inheriting
an internal political situation that was still partially unstable,
as was to be shown by the Pazzi Conspiracy of 1478 – in which
his brother Giuliano was assassinated – but decidedly oriented
toward the definitive consolidation of Medici power.
The rule of the Magnificent coincided with a period of prosperity
and peace in the fragmented political checkerboard of Italy,
thanks to the continuance of that balance of power of which
Lorenzo, called for this reason the "needle in the scales" of Italian
politics, was the chief artificer. His presence, moreover, prevented
the threat of foreign intervention in Italy for as long as he lived.
Under Lorenzo de' Medici Florence reached the height
of its splendor, becoming the cradle of the Italian Renaissance
and the center from which the new civilization radiated.
Himself a poet and man of letters, collector of precious objects
and ancient statues in the famous garden of San Marco
frequented by Leonardo and later by Michelangelo,
Lorenzo fervently promoted artistic and cultural activity.
At his court lived and worked men of letters and philosophers
such as Luigi Pulci, Poliziano, Marsilio Ficino, Cristoforo Landino,
Pico della Mirandola, as well as the greatest artists of the times –
Botticelli, Pollaiolo, Verrocchio, the Ghirlandaio brothers,
the young Leonardo and the very young Michelangelo.

Study from life
for a **Madonna
with the Cat**
(c. 1480-1483),
Florence, Gabinetto Disegni
e Stampe degli Uffizi
(Inv. No. 421 Er).

Study for a
**Madonna
with the Cat**
(c. 1478-1480),
London, British Museum
(Inv. No. 1860-16-98r).

Benois Madonna
(c. 1478-1480),
St. Petersburg,
Hermitage.

The background of the painting, where the thick hedge of juniper thorns (ginepro in Italian) alludes to the name of the model, Ginevra, is symbolic, and is already distinguished by the botanical precision resulting from Leonardo's careful study of the plant world in numerous sketches and drawings executed throughout his lifetime. Leonardo's youthful masterpiece is the *Annunciation* now in the Uffizi. The subject of this painting had a long tradition clearly illustrated in the Tuscan painting of recent times, from Simone Martini to Fra Angelico, to Pollaiolo. But the spatial arrangement of the scene makes of Leonardo's work a sort of oversized predella, rather than an altarpiece of traditional type. Some technical imperfection appearing in this painting has suggested that it may date from the early 1470s.

Based on stylistic affinity with the *Annunciation* in the Louvre, instead, the Uffizi painting has been dated around 1478. In reality it is possible that Leonardo worked on this painting for several years, making it a compendium of everything he had learned in the school of Verrocchio. One of the most striking errors appears in the perspective of the Virgin's right arm, so far back from the lectern that the hand would be unable to reach the book from

that position. In any case the beauty of the figures and the harmony of the ensemble are so superb as to make the few defects in this universally admired painting almost unnoticeable.

The culmination of Leonardo's Florentine years is to be found in another painting now in the Uffizi, the *Adoration of the Magi*. It was painted for a monastery in the vicinity of Florence, San Donato a Scopeto, to which Leonardo's father, Ser

Annunciation
(c. 1475-1478),
whole and detail,
Florence, Uffizi Gallery.

Annunciation
(c. 1478 or 1485),
Paris, Musée du Louvre.

On the two
preceding pages:
Annunciation
(c. 1475-1478), detail,
Florence, Uffizi Gallery.

Filippino Lippi,
**Adoration
of the Magi**
(1496),
Florence, Uffizi Gallery.

Piero da Vinci, lent his services as notary in 1481, the year it was commissioned. In 1482, upon Leonardo's departure for Milan, the artist left the panel unfinished, and the friars of Scopeto had to turn to another painter and wait a good fifteen years to have their church adorned by the *Adoration* altarpiece complete in every part. This was achieved at last by Filippino Lippi who, while using Leonardo's sketch as basis, developed it in a more traditional manner.

The subject of the Adoration was another theme familiar to Tuscan artistic tradition, both previous and contemporary. Leonardo however decidedly renewed it, after long preparation conducted on an extensive series of drawings. Atypically, the

**Adoration
of the Magi**
(c. 1481-1482),
Florence, Uffizi Gallery.

Perspective study
for the background
of the **Adoration
of the Magi**
(c. 1481),
Florence,
Gabinetto Disegni
e Stampe degli Uffizi
(Inv. No. 436).

**Adoration
of the Magi**
(c. 1481-1482), detail,
Florence, Uffizi Gallery.

scene is set outdoors, with the hut of the Nativity off-centered far to the right and only partially visible, as are the ox and the ass. The figures are arranged around the personage of the Virgin, at the center of the composition. The excited movement of their gestures creates a dynamic tension pervading the whole, which has been thought to translate already that interior motion ('moti mentali', or 'mental motion', as Leonardo called it) starting from a propulsive center, which was later to distinguish the *Last Supper* in Milan. In the *Adoration of the Magi*, however, the perspective leads the eye toward a vanishing point which is not central but located between the two trees – the laurel of victory and the palm of martyrdom – at the upper right. It has been observed that, through this stratagem, Leonardo intended

to allude, with a sort of ante litteram cinematic artifice, a sort of imaginary tracking shot that moves from right to left, to an event which had occurred shortly before, namely the Nativity. This event would thus be temporally and ideally incorporated in the other crucial event of the Epiphany. If this is true, then the personage in the foreground on the far right who is looking out of the scene may be considered a self-portrait of Leonardo, the "director", who introduces his creation. A last comment; among the innovative aspects of the *Adoration*, the anatomical concern that was to be foremost in the following years is already clearly apparent. In modeling the individual figures, Leonardo exploited the preparation of the support, creating clear, luminous volumes that emerge from the darker areas shaded in bistre.

The same attention to the anatomy of the human body appears and is even accentuated in another coeval painting, also unfinished, by Leonardo, the *St. Jerome* now in the Pinacoteca Vaticana. Here the saint's body seems a forerunner of the anatomical models drawn thirty years later, around 1510, but in the statuary figure of the hermit the "technical" study comes alive, becomes flesh and blood in an artistically superb personage. In the past this painting underwent numerous vicissitudes. It seems that one of its former owners, Cardinal Fesch, an uncle of Napoleon, bought it – mutilated of the head of St. Jerome – from a rag dealer who had been using it as the cover for a chest. The missing piece was then allegedly found in the shop of a shoemaker, who had been using it as the seat for a stool. The manifest interest in anatomy already appearing in these youthful paintings, which in the Milan years was to be fully and independently developed in a series of significant studies, introduces the question of Leonardo's eclectic personality and of the harmonious presence of a myriad of contemporaneous interests in his research. As a great eclectic genius Leonardo is in some ways comparable to other outstanding figures of the Italian Renaissance – Leon Battista Alberti, Michelangelo, and Raphael. However, the interdisciplinary nature of his studies is more highly accentuated and organic.

His investigations in the various fields of knowledge are in fact more closely connected, often reflected in each other. For example his anatomical, optical and even botanical studies directly influenced his artistic production, so much so that in Leonardo's paintings the portrayal of the human body, the structural elements of the composition and even the representations of plants are not only artistically important in the sense of aesthetics, do not merely satisfy the pre-eminent criteria – especially in the Florentine milieu, dominated by Ficino's Neoplatonism – of beauty and harmony, but also reflect a "scientific" way of looking at the real world. This was confirmed by Leonardo himself when he declared that painting is 'philosophical', that is, in the language of the times, it is scientific. This means that art was for Leonardo one of the possible ways – although a particularly absorbing and sensitive way – of interpreting and faithfully transmitting a knowledge of the perceptible world. At the time of his Florentine apprenticeship Leonardo must have specialized in painting and sculpture, but the crafts of the workshop, as is well known, were many and varied, and it was normal for pupils to experiment with the art of engraving or to learn to solder, to engrave, to cast metals and so on. For Leonardo this may have been a first stimulus to turn toward more technical interests, especially considering that Verrocchio was commissioned

St. Jerome
(c. 1480-1482),
Vatican City,
Pinacoteca Vaticana.

in 1469, the year usually considered the one when the young artist entered the Florentine master's studio, to construct the gilded ball that was to crown the cupola of the Duomo built by Brunelleschi.

It is not improbable that Leonardo collaborated in this undertaking. Certainly he was able to observe the work at first hand, and many years later, in 1515, it was still fresh in his memory: 'Remember the welds used to weld the ball for Santa Maria del Fiore'. It may even be that this was the beginning of his interest in calculation and geometry, aroused by the technical problems involved in producing the ball, as well as in raising it to the top of the dome, where it was placed in 1470. And it is possible that this same experience aroused the curiosity of Verrocchio's young pupil for the machines employed by Brunelleschi (who died in 1446) in the cathedral worksite. This is indicated by the fact that in some of Leonardo's earliest manuscript sheets, datable around the middle of the 1470s, appear drawings of Brunelleschi's devices. These drawings thus seem to constitute, along with some geometric figures, the earliest testimony of Leonardo's widening horizons. As further proof of the artist's early contact with Brunelleschi's technology and inventions there is also a sheet recently discovered in the Uffizi, Gabinetto dei Disegni e delle Stampe [Cabinet of Prints and Drawings], in which an anonymous 16th century artist

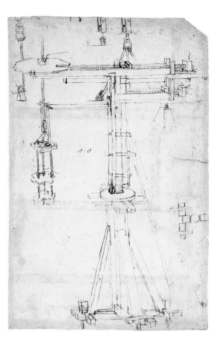

Revolving crane (c. 1478-1480), Codex Atlanticus (f. 965r).

hands down some drawings by Leonardo, most of which have been lost. Among these is one of a boat which calls to mind the legendary "Badalone", the craft invented and patented by Brunelleschi to be used for transporting marble on the Arno River, at the time when the cupola of Santa Maria del Fiore was being built. Stranded in the shallows near Empoli, the "Badalone" may even have been seen by Leonardo, while the boy was living in the nearby town of Vinci. And it would certainly have struck the fervent imagination of that adolescent thirsting for knowledge and adventure.

Boat driven by wind vanes, copy (c. 1530) of lost drawing by Leonardo, Florence, Gabinetto Disegni e Stampe degli Uffizi (Inv. No. 4085).

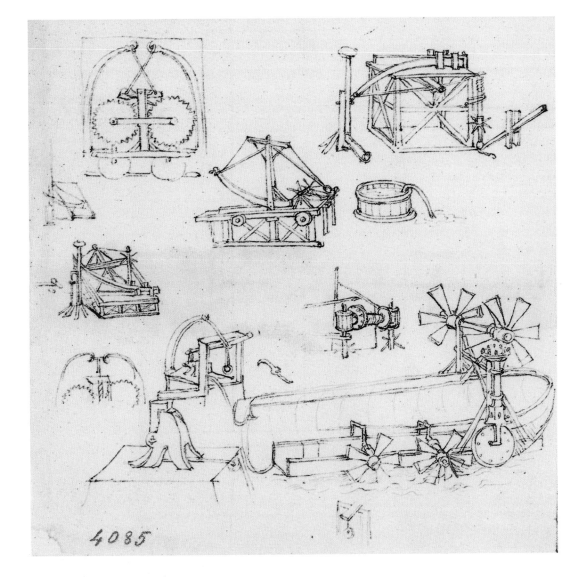

4085

MILAN AND
THE SFORZA COURT

In 1482, as previously mentioned, Leonardo abandoned Florence for Milan. According to the Anonimo Gaddiano, what brought him to the capital of Lombardy was a diplomatic-cultural mission assigned him by Lorenzo de' Medici. To improve his relations with the Duke of Milan Ludovico Sforza, known as "il Moro", Lorenzo sent him by means of Leonardo and the musician Atalante Migliorotti a precious silver lyre in the form of a horse's skull. The event thus seems to fall within the context of cultural exchange promoted by the Magnificent for the purposes of diplomacy, as when

he sent to Rome such artists as Botticelli, Perugino, Ghirlandaio, Piero di Cosimo to work at the Papal courts. The Anonimo Gaddiano writes: '[Leonardo] was thirty years old when he was sent by the said Magnificent Lorenzo to the Duke of Milan [...] to present him with a lyre, which he played like no other'.

This last remark evokes another mythical aspect of Leonardo's eclectic personality, that of musician and inventor of musical instruments linked to still another role, that of master of ceremonies or, as it would be called today, of the ephemeral, where his versatile genius found expression in the organization of festivals and court performances. These interests are demonstrated in the Leonardian codices by

Detail of the facade of Castello Sforzesco at Milan.

drawings of mechanical drums, of wind instruments with keyboards and other musical devices, and by studies of costumes, automata and hydraulic mechanisms for theatrical or sound effects, of which a trace may remain in the decoration of the Sala delle Asse.

For his arrival in Milan, Leonardo had himself preceded by a letter addressed to "il Moro". The letter listed various fields of competence – to the amazing number of thirty-six – in which he believed he could be usefully employed by the Duke of Milan, Ludovico. Emphasis was placed on his capability as military and civil engineer, and also as painter and sculptor. Milan, which was at the time the capital of a rich, modern, dynamic State, was probably seen by Leonardo as the ideal place for his vast range of studies. In 1482 the city was allied with Ferrara in one of those periodic wars which engaged the various Italian States throughout the 15th century, and this undoubtedly made Leonardo's expertise in the military field even more desirable. Leonardo did, in fact, remain in the Lombard capital at the service of Ludovico il Moro, until 1499, when the Duchy was invaded by the troops of Louis XII, King of France. At the service of the Sforza the artist was given a fixed salary as well as a vineyard that had first belonged to the Monastery of San Vittore, situated between Porta Vercellina and the postern of Sant'Ambrogio.

Virgin of the Rocks
(c. 1506-1508),
London, National Gallery.

THE MILAN OF LUDOVICO IL MORO

Ludovico Sforza, known as "il Moro", was the fourth child of Francesco Sforza and Bianca Maria Visconti. In 1476, at the death of Duke Galeazzo Maria, his brother Ludovico began plotting to take over power at the expense of the legitimate heir to the Duchy, the Duke's grandson Gian Galeazzo.
He finally succeeded in 1480, by having himself appointed tutor of his nephew and eliminating dangerous adversaries such as the secretary of State Cicco Simonetta and his sister-in-law Bona di Savoia.
But his de facto government was opposed by the wife of the inept Gian Galeazzo, Isabella d'Aragon, supported by her uncle the King of Naples. Growing friction with the Kingdom of Naples finally induced "il Moro" to advocate the intervention in Italy, in 1494, of the French King Charles VIII, who claimed his right to the Aragonese throne.
But the appeal to the King of France was also to bring about the downfall of the Sforza dynasty, since in 1499 the new French King, Louis XII, invaded the Duchy of Milan, conquering it. In the capital of his rich, industrious State, "il Moro" and his ambitious wife, Beatrice d'Este, promoted a culture which could be called "imported", engaging for the prestige of the court great engineers mainly from other regions, first among them Leonardo and Bramante.

Master of the
Pala Sforzesca,
Sforzesca Altarpiece
(c. 1494-1495),
detail with Ludovico
il Moro, Milan,
Pinacoteca di Brera.

On facing page:
painted decoration
of the Sala delle Asse
(c. 1498),
Milan,
Castello Sforzesco.

Virgin of the Rocks
(c. 1483-1485),
whole and detail,
Paris, Museé du Louvre.

In Milan Leonardo took lodgings in the neighborhood of Porta Ticinese with the de' Predis brothers, the artists who painted the side panels (now in London) of the Louvre *Virgin of the Rocks*, which was his first Milanese painting. The work was commissioned of Leonardo in 1483 by the Confraternity of the Immaculate Conception for the church – now destroyed – of San Francesco Grande. A haunting scenario of rocks, from which comes the title – scattered with clumps of plants all really existing and painted by the artist with botanical precision forms the background to the group of the Virgin with Child, the infant St. John the Baptist and an angel with a supremely gentle expression. The enigmatic iconography and the hermetic nature of the panel, undoubtedly linked to the mysterious dogma of the Immaculate Conception, the name of the brotherhood which commissioned the painting, are still today the subject of heated debate.

The most famous of the paintings executed by Leonardo in Milan – the *Last Supper* frescoed in Santa Maria delle Grazie – also has a sacred subject. But during his stay at the court of Ludovico il Moro the supremely talented artist also painted extraordinary works of profane subject in which personages of the Sforza court are admirably depicted.

THE PORTRAITS
AND THE "LAST SUPPER"

Dating from around 1485 is the *Portrait of a Musician*, generally considered to portray the choir master of the Milan Cathedral, Franchino Gaffurio. While in the sculptural rendering of the figure the Tuscan influence is still evident, in the colors, the composition and the dark, uniform background can be seen instead the influence of Flemish portraiture mediated by Antonello da Messina. Masterly is the rendering of the eyes with their glassy reflections, the result of careful study, appearing as the 'window of the soul' (the expression is that of Leonardo himself) and forming the focal point of the composition.

Graceful and at the same time powerful are the two portraits of women, the *Lady with an Ermine* and *La belle Ferronnière*, both unforgettable for their concision and forceful representation. Here Leonardo experimented with the so-called "shoulder portrait", perfected in various studies on the dynamic and plastic potentialities of the human body, of which a significant example remains at Windsor, where a woman's bust, observed all-round, is portrayed from eighteen different viewpoints. *The Lady with an Ermine* is a portrait of the eighteen-year-old mistress of the Duke of Milan, Cecilia Gallerani.

Portrait of a Musician (c. 1485), whole and detail, Milan, Pinacoteca Ambrosiana.

**Lady
with an Ermine
(Portrait
of Cecilia
Gallerani)**
(c. 1485),
whole and detail,
Cracow, Czartoryski
Muzeum.

La Belle Ferronnière
(c. 1495),
Paris, Musée du Louvre.

The ermine (in Greek "galè") which the young woman holds in her arms alludes to her name, just as the juniper bush referred to Ginevra Benci in the portrait of the Florentine lady. But still more; the little animal, endowed with many symbolic meanings, traditionally alluded also to candor and moderation. Lastly, it evoked Ludovico il Moro himself, called 'the Italian Moor, white ermine' in a sonnet dedicated to this painting by the court poet Bernardo Bellincioni in 1493. Moreover, the Duke had been awarded the high honor of the Ordine dell'Armellino, conferred on him by the King of Naples between 1488 and 1490, the time in which the portrait was probably painted.

La Belle Ferronnière was instead dedicated to another favorite of "il Moro". She was presumably Lucrezia Crivelli, who took the place of Cecilia Gallerani in the favor of the Duke. The title of the painting, dated around 1495, was erroneously conferred on it in the 18th century, when it was thought

Study of head of
Bartholomew
for the **Last Supper**
(c. 1495),
Windsor (RL 12548).

Study of composition
for the **Last Supper**
(1493-1494),
Venice, Gallerie
dell'Accademia
(Inv. No. 254).

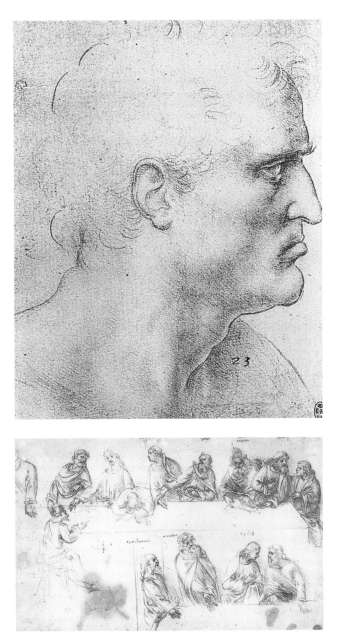

to portray not the mistress of Ludovico Sforza but of the King of France François I. The woman is thought by some experts to have been the wife of a certain Le Ferron, by others instead the wife of an iron merchant, as would be indicated by the literal translation of the word "ferronnière". Curiously enough, in the early 19th century the painting contributed to launching the fashion of a chain (or ribbon) with a precious stone at the center, worn on the forehead like Leonardo's beautiful model, and called for this reason "ferronnière".

But the most important and famous work painted by Leonardo during his first stay in Milan is, as previously mentioned, the *Last Supper* in Santa Maria delle Grazie. This monumental wall painting was begun around 1495 and certainly completed before 1498, when the mathematician Luca Pacioli mentioned it in the dedicatory letter of his *De divina proportione* addressed to Ludovico il Moro. As regards the origins of this painting,

clear references are lacking. On the one hand, contemporary documentation on the client and on the reasons behind this ambitious project is totally lacking; on the other, very few preparatory studies have survived. As regards iconography, interesting testimony was furnished many years later, in 1517, by Antonio de Beatis, secretary of Cardinal Louis d'Aragon, who on the morrow of his meeting with Leonardo at Amboise

stated that the master had confided in him that the figures in the *Last Supper* portrayed personages in the Sforza court as well as people from the street, the latter being confirmed also by some notes made by Leonardo himself. In addition, a certain source of inspiration for the figures of Christ and the Apostles was undoubted the hagiographic tradition, primarily that of the New Testament. Moreover, the artist probably

Last Supper
(c. 1495-1497),
whole and detail of Christ,
Milan, refectory of the
Convent of Santa Maria
delle Grazie.

der a preparatory drawing for the *Last Supper* on a sheet now at Windsor. One of the aspects that seems to faithfully follow the New Testament account is the setting. In fact, before the floor of the refectory was substantially raised, the scene appeared to have been painted from a point of view six meters high, on the level of the second floor that would normally have contained, in a typical Mediterranean building of the 1st century AD, the room described by Mark and Luke (XIV, 15 and XXII, 12). It should also be recalled that Leonardo, while taking into account the previous pictorial tradition – from Taddeo Gaddi to Andrea del Castagno, to Ghirlandaio – rejected the iconography utilized by most of the artists who had confronted the theme of the *Last Supper*, refusing to portray Judas isolated on the other side of the banquet table. The betraying Apostle is in fact shown among his companions, six on each side of Christ, rhythmically subdivided into groups of three. This decision may have been conditioned by an explicit request of the Dominicans, the order to which the monastery of Santa Maria delle Grazie belonged. This order made free will a fundamental theme of its preaching, and it is probably to illustrate Dominican thought on this point that Judas is presented on the same level as the other personages, like one who, being

Last Supper,
(c. 1495-1497),
details before and after
restoration, Milan, refectory
of the Convent of Santa
Maria delle Grazie.

Last Supper
detail of apostle Matthew.

made good use of his early studies of physiognomy, closely linked to those of anatomy, to render the range and the shades of feelings and emotions, the famous 'moti mentali'. 'When you draw a figure, consider well who it is and what you want it to do', wrote Leonardo un-

Domenico del Ghirlandaio,
Last Supper
(1480),
Florence, former
monastery of Ognissanti.

able to choose between good and evil, voluntarily decides to do evil. Evidently it would have been judged incorrect to portray the guilty Judas already outside of the group, as one "predestined" without appeal. Confirmation that this iconography originated in the Dominican milieu seems to come from other paintings of the same subject destined to the monasteries of the order, for example the *Last Supper* by Fra Angelico for the Silverware Cupboard in the Monastery of San Marco in Florence.

Because of the technique employed – tempera paint over two layers of preparation, but not applied "a fresco", on the still wet wall – and due to the dampness of the wall, the *Last Supper* underwent early deterioration that irrep-

arably damaged its legibility. Its first restoration dates from the 18th century, while the latest radical cleaning was carried out in the years 1978 to 1999, restoring long-lost colors and details.

Another work from the artist's first stay in Milan which was intended to be equally grandiose but which was instead never completed is the equestrian monument to Francesco Sforza, which was to have celebrated the founding father of the dynasty. The project was highly ambitious. It called for a grandiose statue even larger than those, already exceptional, of the two most famous contemporary monuments of this kind, that of the Gattamelata executed by Donatello at Padova and that of Bartolomeo Colleoni realized at Venice by Leonardo's former

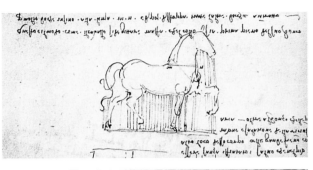

Study for the casting of the equestrian monument to Francesco Sforza (c. 1493), Codex Madrid II (f. 149r), detail.

Andrea del Verrocchio, **Equestrian Monument to Bartolomeo Colleoni** (1479), Venice, Campo dei Santi Giovanni e Paolo.

master, Verrocchio. In Leonardo's group, in fact, the horse alone was to have been six meters high. The artist worked fervently on the Sforza Monument for years, preparing a clay model of the horse in natural size and completing, in collaboration with the mathematician Luca Pacioli, the necessary calculations for the bronze casting. But the efforts of a decade came to naught due to the French invasion of 1499. The troops of Louis XII destroyed the model of the horse, while Leonardo departed from Milan to return to Florence.

Up to this point we have focused on the artistic production of the Tuscan master at the service of "il Moro". But Leonardo's activity in the field of art accounts for only a small part of his achievements during these years. In fact, just as had been guaranteed in the letter to the Duke, the eclectic thirty-year-old from Tuscany was destined to play numerous roles at the Sforza court, his research ranging contemporaneously over many fields.

Study of rearing horse
and rider trampling
a fallen enemy
(c. 1490),
Windsor (RL 12358).

Neptune with Horses
(c. 1503-1504),
Windsor (RL 12570).

THE "LOVE OF BOYS": LEONARDO AND HOMOSEXUALITY

In 1476, at the time of his apprenticeship with Verrocchio, Leonardo underwent a trial for sodomy, which however concluded with his acquittal. The mention of this episode serves to introduce the theme of Leonardo's presumed homosexuality, a subject long avoided and often denied, as pointed out by Freud in his essay on the artist written in 1910. For the Viennese physician, the sexual diversity of the master from Vinci was taken for granted and was linked, through the psychoanalytic approach then being developed, to the artist's infancy and childhood.
Leonardo's homosexuality is explicitly mentioned in a much older text, the *Libro dei sogni* (*Book of Dreams*), written by the Lombard painter and theoretician Giovan Paolo Lomazzo around 1560, only forty years or so after the death of the artist. In this poetic fiction, it is Leonardo himself to speak of his particular relationship with Salaì, remarking that he was the pupil whom 'in life I loved more than all the others who were different' and shortly afterward going into a long discourse 'on the love of boys' which is a real dissertation in praise of homosexuality, illustrated by classic examples and salacious remarks. In the same *Libro dei sogni* Leonardo, claiming for Florence a sort of "supremacy" of sodomy, makes an allusion to Perugino, who had been his very young companion in Verrocchio's workshop. In the *Cronaca rimata* written by Giovanni Santi (Raphael's father) around 1488, the author mentioned the two apprentices Leonardo and Perugino as 'two youths equal in station and in love'.

Adoration of the Magi (c. 1481-1482), detail, Florence, Uffizi Gallery;
the young man portrayed may be a self-portrait of Leonardo at the age of thirty.

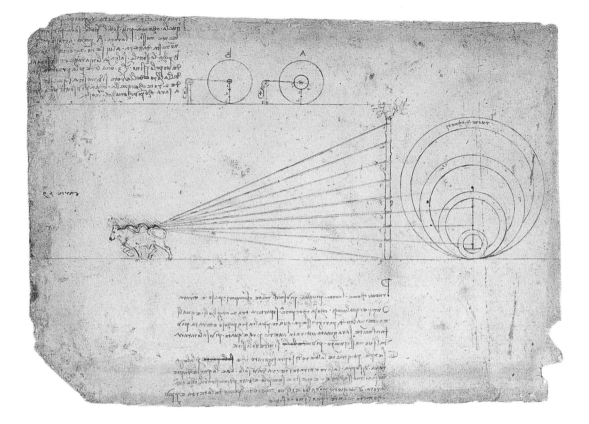

ENGINEERING AND ARCHITECTURAL WORKS

One of Leonardo's basic occupations was that of Ducal engineer. In this capacity he engaged in civil and military architecture and problems "on the territory", although in these sectors his commitment may have gone no further than consultation and proposals, since it is impossible to know precisely what he may have achieved in the practical field. Leonardo's first known architectural studies date from the Milanese period. Of his youthful projects, in fact, the only remaining traces are to be found in the writings of Vasari, who recalls the project, never carried out, for lifting the Florentine Baptistery and placing it on a polygonal base. The master's drawings

Geometric proportions applied to the study of traction (c. 1487-1490), Codex Atlanticus (f. 561).

Study of church
with central plan
(c. 1487-1489),
Manuscript B (f. 95r).

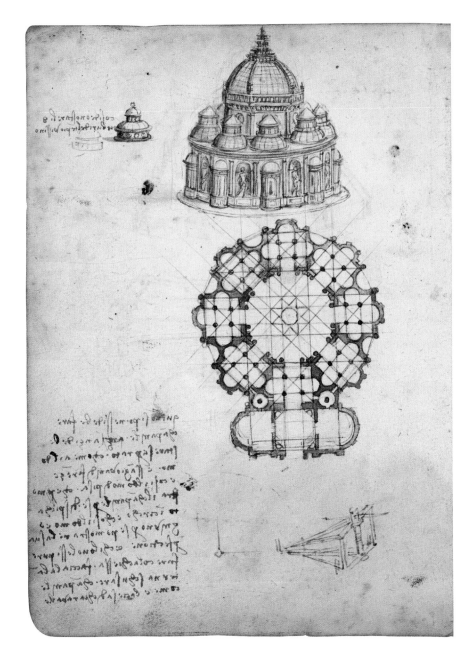

for the lantern of the Milan Cathedral date from the two-year period 1488-1490. To these may be added a series of proposals and reflections on churches with circular layout, which may be linked to discussions with great experienced architects such as Bramante and Giuliano da Sangallo, also working in the Lombardy capital at that time. Contemporaneously, Leonardo developed models of military constructions, as in the projects for the fortifications of Milan, of Vigevano and of Pavia which appear partially influenced by the greatest military architect of the times, Francesco di Giorgio Martini.

As previously stated, the practical consequences of these studies are unknown. It is instead certain that the designing of architectural models opened the way for the artist toward other fields of study. As in a sort of "avalanche effect", Leonardo seems to have been stimulated, regardless of the subject which absorbed him at any particular moment, by an inexhaustible intellectual curiosity that led him from one thing to another in a process of continuous discovery and deepening research. For example, the architectural projects were to lead to his studies of building statics, while new interests sprang continuously from other projects and problems on which he worked during his stay in Milan. Moreover, the invention of military ma-

Study of cranium
(c. 1489),
Windsor (RL 19058v).

chines and even machines for industrial use – especially in the field of textiles, in keeping with the traditional development of the textile industry in Lombardy – was a design activity that was to stimulate his studies in mechanics. Or the development of hydraulic works, a new field that Leonardo now approached inevitably in a region where the problem of exploiting water by channeling it usefully had always been a primary concern, and where a vast network of canals already spread throughout the territory. This led to Leonardo's interest in water, and his studies on hydraulics and hydrostatics.

In relation to the various problems and the new challenges arising from his multifold activities, Leonardo approached, during his years in Milan, the most diverse fields of research, deepening his knowledge of subjects which he had only touched upon before. One of these was the study of Latin, resumed in order to approach, he the 'man without letters', the great texts of the classical scientific tradition and the treatises of the Humanists; and, from 1496, when the mathematician Luca Pacioli also entered the service of "il Moro", geometry, which Leonardo began to study again with the aid of the Franciscan monk, illustrating the treatise of the latter, *De divina proportione*. And again, in around 1489-1490, Leonardo dedicated himself to his first important studies of anatomy, starting

Study of cranium
(c. 1489),
Windsor (RL 19058r).

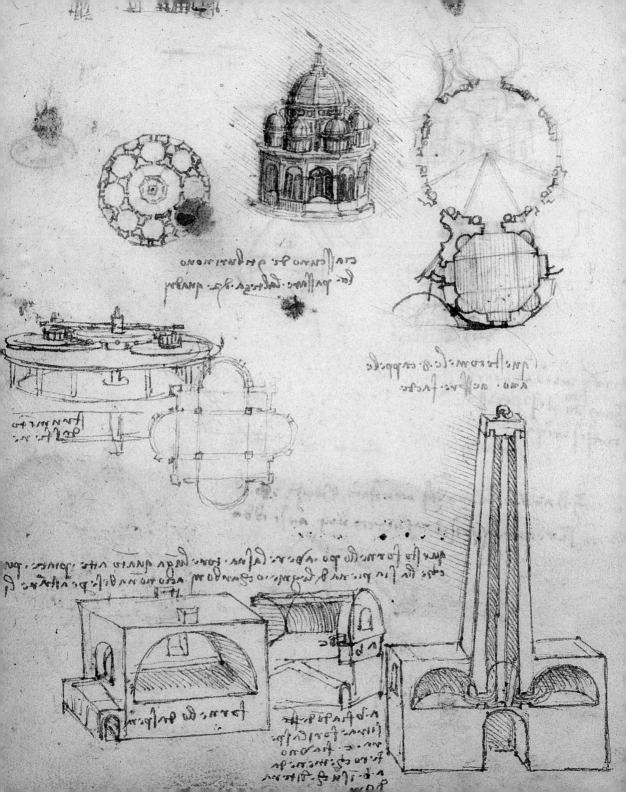

Study of thrust
on arches for the lantern
of the Milan Cathedral
(c. 1487-1490),
Codex Atlanticus
(f. 850r).

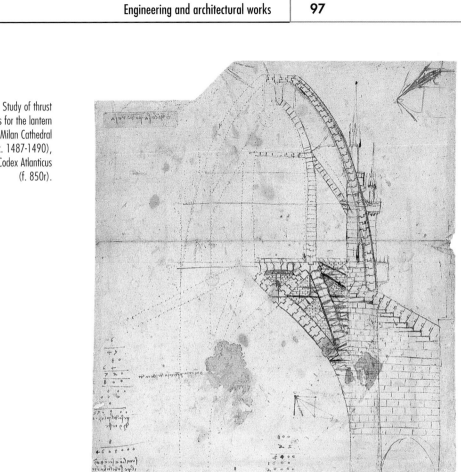

Studies of circular churches,
of reverberatory furnaces
and of a "ball instrument"
(c. 1487-1489),
Manuscript B
(f. 21v), detail.

from the drawings of craniums now in the Windsor collection. Lastly, he developed his interest in flight and the construction of flying machines, which had made its first timid appearance already near the end of the Florentine period, as demonstrated by some sketches on a sheet in the Uffizi which also contains a study for the *Adoration of the Magi*. Along with the forceful emerging of a new mass of interests

so copious and wide-ranging, Leonardo began to feel the impelling need, starting just in those Milanese years, of continuously annotating his reflections, projects and studies. From this time on the scattered sheets were to be accompanied by notebooks, the earliest known ones being those called the Codex Trivulziano and the Manuscript B of France, both compiled in Milan starting from 1487.

LEONARDO'S SCHOOL

Marco d'Oggiono,
The Holy Children
(c. 1500).

During his first stay in Milan, Leonardo gathered around him
several pupils, among them the famous Salaì (or Salaino),
the 'little demon', as Giovanni Giacomo Caprotti was nicknamed
for his impetuous nature and frequent thefts.
He 'came to stay with me on the day of the Magdalene in 1490,
at the age of 10', records the master in a note from 1491.
In addition to Salaì and other apprentices the Vincian Academy
also welcomed, unlike the traditional art workshops of the times –
and somewhat on the model of Ficini's Florentine Platonic Academy
– masters who had already reached success. Among the illustrious
names of the Leonardian school are the Evangelista brothers
and Ambrogio de' Predis, Francesco Napolitano, Marco
d'Oggiono, Andrea Solario and Giovan Antonio Boltraffio.
The latter two in particular faithfully interpreted the lesson taught
by Leonardo, especially in portraits, the genre in which
the Vincian Academy was highly specialized.
The emblem of the Vincian Academy, as demonstrated
by six splendid prints, are the so-called 'Vincian knots',
complicated interwoven decorative devices which may have
inspired the intertwined plant motifs in the Sala delle Asse.

Giovan Antonio Boltraffio,
**Symbolic Portrait on the
Theme of St. Sebastian**
(c. 1500),
Moscow, Museo Puškin.

Giovan Antonio Boltraffio,
Symbolic Portrait
(c. 1500),
Florence, Uffizi Gallery.

Andrea Solario,
**Madonna of the
Green Cushion**
(c. 1507),
Paris, Musée du Louvre.

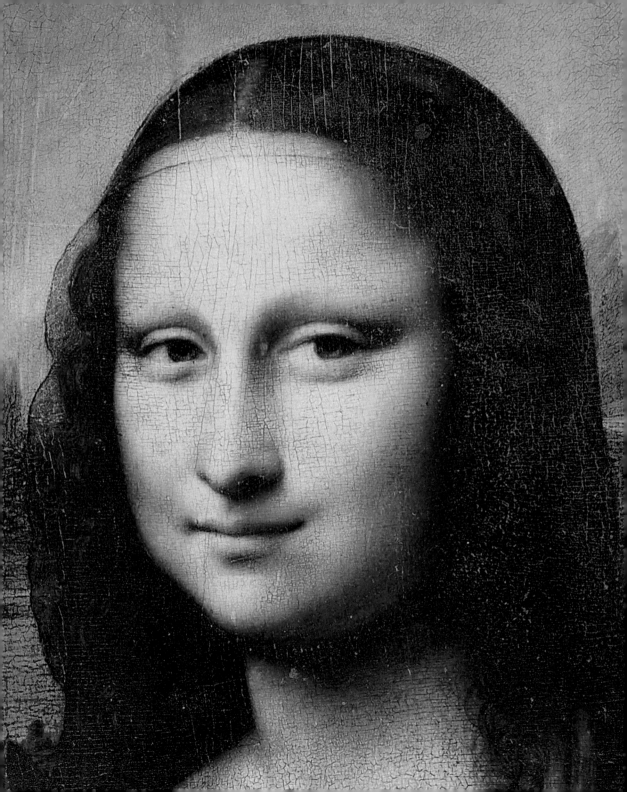

1500/1519 **Maturity**

RETURN TO FLORENCE

In 1499 Leonardo left the Duchy of Milan, invaded by French troops, and took the road that led back to Florence. These are the brief words with which, in 1500, he commented on the downfall of Ludovico il Moro, in whose service he had remained for a period which was to be longer than any spent with the various rulers for whom he worked: 'The Duke has lost the State and his property and his freedom, and no work will be finished for him'.

In his journey of return to the former city of the Medici, which had been proclaimed a Republic in 1494, Leonardo made a first stop in Mantova, at the residence of Isabella d'Este. Wife of Francesco II Gonzaga and sister of the Duchess of Milan, Beatrice, who had married Ludovico il Moro and died in childbirth in 1497, the Marquise di Mantova was the leader of one of the most refined and exclusive courts of the Italian Renaissance. For her Leonardo drew a famous portrait in charcoal, promising to transfer it soon to a panel painting, a promise that was never fulfilled. After Mantova came Venice where, probably due to the fame he had won in Milan as hydraulic engineer, Leonardo was commissioned by the Serenissima Republic to devise a plan for flooding an area particularly exposed to the raids of the Turks, whose incursions the glorious Republic feared more deeply with every day that passed.

Upon arriving in Florence the artist first lodged with the Servite Brothers in the Monastery of the Santissima Annunziata. Later he went to live in the home of the mathematician Piero di Braccio Martelli, not far from the Duomo and

**Portrait of
Isabella d'Este**
(c. 1499-1500),
Paris, Musée du Louvre,
Département des Arts
Graphiques (inv. MI 753).

from the Medici Palace. During this new stay in Florence, Leonardo's existence was enlivened by the customary multifold interests that had already emerged in Milan. But now research in the technical and scientific field clearly prevailed over artistic concerns. This was noted in 1501 by Isabella d'Este's agent in Florence, Pietro da Novellara, who in his letters to the Marchese reports that Leonardo could no longer stand the sight of a paintbrush, being totally absorbed in mathematical studies: '[Leonardo] is working hard on geometry [...] and is most impatient with the brush'; and still further: 'His mathematical experiments have so far distracted him from painting that he can no longer stand to see a brush'. And in effect, Leonardo's works during this return to Florence were very few – few, but important.

Michelangelo Buonarroti,
David
(1501-1504),
Florence,
Galleria dell'Accademia.

FROM SIGNORIA TO REPUBLIC

In 1494 the invasion of Italy by the French King Charles VIII marked the onset of the future foreign domination of the peninsula. But the immediate consequences of this event were also important. In Florence for example, the invasion of the King of France determined the expulsion of Piero de' Medici, the son and successor of Lorenzo the Magnificent, and the establishment of a theocratic republic headed by Girolamo Savonarola. For four years the Dominican friar dominated the city's politics with his intransigent principles and his ideas for radical reform of public and private morality. But having fallen into disgrace after being excommunicated by Pope Alexander VI, Savonarola was burned at the stake as a heretic in 1498. The Florentine Republic did not, however, die with him, but evolved toward a government headed by a Gonfaloniere elected for life, in whose hands power was concentrated. In 1502 Pier Soderini was elected to this office. With him, cultural initiatives and commissions to artists, severely curtailed under the rule of Savonarola, began to flourish again. It was under Soderini's government, in fact, that Leonardo and Michelangelo were commissioned to paint the unfinished Battles in Palazzo Vecchio and that Michelangelo sculpted the David, elected symbol of the young Republic, which lasted until 1512, when events linked to the Holy Alliance against the French invoked by Pope Julius II brought the Medici back to Florence.

Study of cartoon for
Saint Anne
(c. 1501),
Venice, Gallerie
dell'Accademia
(Inv. No. 230).

Study for a
Kneeling Leda
(1503-1504),
Chatsworth,
Duke of Devonshire
Collection (Inv. No. 717).

To begin with was the first cartoon, lost, for the *Saint Anne* executed in 1501. This cartoon – it is again Novellara reporting – presented some important changes as compared to the one of 1508, now in London. Differing were in fact the arrangement of the figures and the presence of the lamb as explicit symbol of the Passion. In the London drawing the lamb is replaced by the less patently allusive figure of the infant St. John the Baptist, but appears again in the unfinished painting now in the Louvre begun around 1510.

Then comes the *Madonna of the Yarn Winders*, of which two versions survive, attributed to pupils of Leonardo, with the assistance of the master. This

Leonardo and assistants,
**Madonna
of the Yarn Winders**
(c. 1501).

work was painted for the Secretary of State of Louis XII, Florimond Robertet, as reported again by Novellara.

A first elaboration of the *Leda*, symbol of Prolific Nature, now appeared in drawings and studies carried out around 1504, portraying a kneeling figure. Subsequently, in Milan, the artist was to arrive at a version in which the figure is standing, as proven by the surviving works of the Leonardesque school which reiterate the subject. Lastly, the most important work, the grandiose *Battle of Anghiari* – three times the size of the *Last Supper* – was commissioned of Leonardo in 1503 by the Florentine government to recall a glorious episode in the history of the Republic, the victory over the Milanese in 1440. Such an important commission must have represented for the master the acknowledgement of his now consolidated fame, but it was also an open challenge from the other supreme artist of those years, Michelangelo. In fact, the *Battle of Anghiari* was to be painted in the Great Council Hall (later the Hall of the Five Hundred) in Palazzo Vecchio where, on the wall opposite Leonardo's painting, Michelangelo had been invited to paint the *Battle of Cascina* at the same time. To our great misfortune, neither of the two works was completed. Michelangelo prepared only the cartoon, which has been lost, and then left in 1506 for

paints and was not that of frescoing, perhaps because painting on a still wet wall called for great rapidity, incompatible with Leonardo's slow rhythms. The paint, unable to dry fast enough, began to drip disastrously. In 1506 Leonardo was still working on the *Battle* when he had to abandon it, called to Milan by Charles d'Amboise. In the same year that Michelangelo departed from Florence, Leonardo left the Tuscan capital. Since the cartoon for the *Battle of Anghiari* has been lost and everything Leonardo had painted on the wall of the hall disappeared in 1563 under the paintings of Vasari, the memory of that work is transmitted today only by copies, the most famous of which is the so-called *Doria Panel*.

Leonardo da Vinci (?), **Doria Panel** (c. 1504), Florence, Opificio delle Pietre Dure, copy of the central part of Leonardo's cartoon for the **Battle of Anghiari**, the only portion transferred to the wall and then lost, whole and detail.

Rome, where he remained in the service of the Pope. Leonardo managed instead to transfer to the wall the central part of his cartoon, which used oil paints and has also been lost. However the results were even more disastrous than for the *Last Supper*. Again this was due to the technique employed, which used oil

It should however be recalled again that in his second Florentine period Leonardo was occupied not so much by painting as by scientific studies, a

Cross-section of a leg (c. 1510), Windsor (RL 12627).

Studies on solid geometry and polyhedrons (1505), Codex Forster I (ff. 13r and 13v).

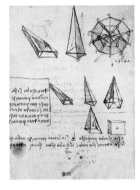

passion for geometry and anatomy, the study of flight and of water. At his side was once again Luca Pacioli, who came with him to Florence from Milan, and who was then preparing, among other things, a new edition of the writings of Euclid, to be published in Venice in 1509.

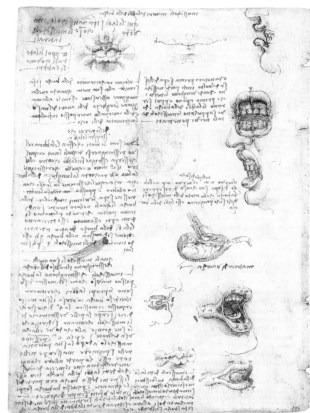

First studies for the **Battle of Anghiari** (c. 1503-1504), Venice, Gallerie dell'Accademia (Inv. No. 215).

Studies on muscles of the mouth (c. 1508), Windsor (RL 19055v).

As for the anatomical studies, Leonardo's first documented dissection of a corpse took place in the winter of 1507-1508. Of his fundamentally important experience in dissecting the corpse of an old man who died in Florence, he notes in his writings: 'This old man, a few hours before his death, told me he was over a hundred years old, and that he felt no failure in his person apart from weakness, and thus lying on a bed in the Hospital of Santa Maria Nova in Florence, with no other movement or sign of any accident, he departed this life […]. His anatomy I described very diligently and with great ease, since the old man had no fat nor humors, which greatly hinders recognition of the parts'. Obviously, the different approach to studying the human body and the diffusion of the practice of dissection, which began to

Birds exploiting
air currents
in their gliding flight
(c. 1505),
Codex on the
Flight of Birds (f. 8r).

ale. Around the same date he conceived the idea of a flying machine, a sort of modern hang glider with which to take flight from the top of Mount Ceceri at Fiesole, in the vicinity of Florence. Linked to the studies of flight is the crucial discovery of spiral motion, recognized by Leonardo as one of the vital forces of nature and immediately studied in other natural phenomena, such as whirlpools in water, the motion of the blood and even of the hair, through a comparative procedure repeatedly adopted by him. And that same spiral motion entered Leonardo's artistic language as well, probably suggesting the twisting of the *Leda* and the impetuous confusion of the *Battle of Anghiari*. These twisting lines were to make of Leonardo, along with Michelangelo and his serpentine figures, one of the models for Mannerist art.

Dating from this second Florentine period was a bold project never carried out: the deviation of the course of the Arno River. The channel imagined by Leonardo was to have passed through Prato and Pistoia, roughly following the course of today's Firenze-Mare superhighway, to join the river again in the vicinity of Pisa. The project offered the dual advantage of making the Arno navigable from Florence to the sea, and allowing the river to flow through important parts of the territory under Florentine influence. Curiously

spread just in those years, marked a great step forward for the art of Leonardo and that of the Renaissance in general, influencing its greatest artists, first among them Michelangelo.

His studies of flight also underwent great progress during those years in Florence. Tenaciously Leonardo observed the behavior of the birds in the wind, describing this around 1505 in a little codex now in the Turin Biblioteca Reenough, it should be mentioned that, while clear traces of this proposal of Leonardo's for "pacific" aims remain, we can instead only conjecture as to the role it may have played in the similar "war plan" (promoted by Niccolò Machiavelli) which the Florentine Republic intended to implement (but failed to do so) to subjugate the rebellious town of Pisa. In this case too the course of the Arno was to be deviated, but in such a way as to cut off the besieged city from its outlet to the sea. During the years when he returned to live in Florence, Leonardo did not always reside in the city. From 1500 to 1502 his presence there was most stable, except for brief absences such as a journey to Rome. In the summer of 1502 he took an important decision, leaving the Tuscan capital to enter the service of Cesare Borgia, known as "il Valentino", the natural son of Pope Alexander VI. Leonardo's appointment to the position of 'Prestantissimo e Dilettissimo Familiare Architetto e Ingegnere Generale' of "il Valentino" was a true investiture, certified by a patent in writing. Perhaps the two had met in Milan, where Cesare Borgia had triumphantly entered with Louis XII of France. On behalf of "il Valentino", Leonardo departed to inspect the territories which the "Duke of Romagna" had occupied in Central Italy, and then followed him in his

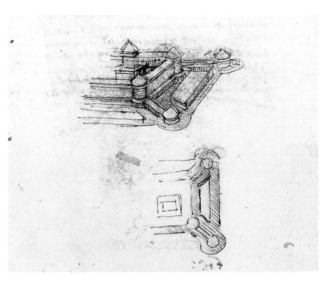

military campaigns through Emilia Romagna, Marche, Umbria and Tuscany. The inspection of cities, fortresses and districts led to some important geographical charts, among them the stupendous sheets in color with the *Map of Imola* and the *Hydrographic chart of Tuscany* showing the course of the Arno. By the spring of 1503, even before "il Valentino's" adventure ended with the dissolution of his dreams and his dominion, Leonardo had already returned to Florence. Here the Republic commissioned of him, as has been seen, the painting of the *Battle of Anghiari*. Then in 1506 he departed again for Milan, for another long stay broken by temporary returns to the Tuscan capital until 1508.

Birds-eye view of fortress (c. 1504), Codex Madrid II, (f. 79r).

LEONARDO AND MICHELANGELO

The well-known rivalry between Leonardo and Michelangelo was due both
to the conflict between different generations (Leonardo was twenty-three years older than Michelangelo) and to a different mentality and irreconcilable artistic concepts:
on the one hand Leonardo's rationality, his rigorously scientific bent and the priority he assigned to painting, on the other Michelangelo's deep spirituality and his firm conviction of the superiority of sculpture.
A manuscript written near the middle of the 16th century, the Anonimo Magliabechiano, reports the amusing episode of a clash between the two greatest Italian artists of the day
in the public street during the time when they were both in Florence working on the paintings in Palazzo Vecchio.
The Magliabechiano Manuscript relates:
'The said Leonardo happening to walk with Giovanni da Gavine from Santa Trinita […] where a group of gentlemen had gathered to discuss a passage from Dante, they called Leonardo asking him to explain to them that passage […] And Michele Agnolo happened to be passing by, and was greeted by one of them; Leonardo answered: "Michele Agnolo himself will explain it to you". Since it seemed to Michelangelo that this had been said to ridicule him, he answered angrily: "Explain it yourself, you who made a drawing of a horse to have a bronze cast [the equestrian statue of Francesco Sforza never completed] and you could not cast it and for shame you left it there". And having said this he turned his back and strode off, leaving Leonardo standing there, blushing at those words'.

Michelangelo,
Virgin with Child and Saint Anne
(c. 1501-1502),
copy from Leonardo,
Oxford, Ashmolean Museum.

THE SECOND STAY IN MILAN

Leonardo went to Milan in 1506 at the urgent request of the French Governor Charles d'Amboise. Since the artist was still at that time at the service of the government of Florence, a quarrel arose with the Florentine Signoria which in the end, at the direct request of the King of France, decided to release the artist from his commitments, allowing him to settle definitively in Milan in 1508.

Here Leonardo remained until 1513, practically in the employment of King Louis XII, who also returned to him the vineyard of San Vittore, confiscated at the time of the French conquest of the Duchy. It was probably in that same 1499 that the artist entered into contact with the King. In any case, it is certain that in 1501 Leonardo was already working for the French, as has been seen by the reference to the *Madonna of the Yarn Winders* made by Isabella d'Este's correspondent in Florence.

Having definitively returned to Milan, Leonardo developed some of his ideas from the Florentine years, such as the previously mentioned paintings of the *Leda* and the *Saint Anne*. The artist probably continued to work on them even during his stay in France, a hypothesis that for the latter of these two

**Virgin with Saint Anne
and the Child
(The Burlington
House Cartoon)**
(c. 1508-1510),
London, National Gallery
(Inv. No. NG6337).

**Saint Anne,
the Virgin
and the Child
with a Lamb**
(c. 1510-1513),
Paris, Musée
du Louvre.

ANATOMICAL STUDIES

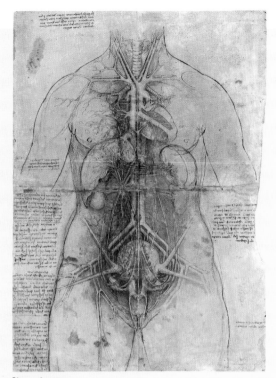

Situs viscerum
(c. 1510),
Windsor (RL 12281).

In the field of anatomical drawing Leonardo achieved the finest results ever attained up to that time.
His drawings are clear, precise and beautiful. Such mastery derived from the practice of dissection, which Leonardo was one of the first to use systematically, although in the past other artists of the Florentine Quattrocento, such as Leonardo's master Andrea del Verrocchio and Antonio del Pollaiolo, had almost certainly had some experience with it. But Leonardo's anatomical drawings are not only admirable, they are above all useful, insofar as they visually explain many things so complicated that it would be hard to describe them verbally. The artist was well aware of this when he wrote: 'O writer, with what letters can you write with such perfection the entire figuration as the drawing does?' The use of illustration of the highest quality is in effect Leonardo's greatest contribution to the scientific writings of the 16th century, while his studies were not, instead, so important for progress in medical science.
In other words, the results he achieved in the anatomical field resembled those in the other fields of his research, that is, his work represented the culminating peak of a process already begun, rather than a total innovation. The traditional image of Leonardo as isolated genius and pioneer free from any debt to the past should thus be reappraised.
Proof is provided by the fact that Leonardo's interest in anatomy sprang from the revolution that had taken place in the 15th century in the representation of pictorial space with the invention of perspective.

The perspective rendering of the body, its three-dimensional nature, had in fact become important, leading to the desire for a thorough knowledge of the structure and functioning of every part. Anatomical knowledge had thus become functional to artistic representation, and the artist became the key illustrator of the progress achieved by anatomy. This was, moreover, one of the aspects of that synthesis of science and art characteristic of the new Renaissance season, an integration which Leonardo interpreted supremely throughout his career.

Anonymous
from Leonardo,
Leda
(c. 1505-1507),
Florence, Uffizi Gallery.

carnal ones of a Bacchus, although not as openly equivocal as in the painting by Caravaggio. On close consideration of the image, it would seem that the *St. John* presents an ambiguity of sexual nature. The impression conveyed is that of a hermaphrodite, to which Leonardo seems to allude in knowing, self-satisfied manner, displaying the fusion of the sexes in a single body. This fusion had already had a significant forerunner in the androgynous figure of a lost *Angel of the Annunciation* of which some school replicas remain, the best of which is now in Basel, as well as in a sketch drawn by the hand of a pupil and retouched by Leonardo on a sheet dating from around 1504. An even more striking example of ambiguity can be seen in the erotic-demoniacal figure, it too midway between Bacchus and an angel, of a youth with erect penis, the *"Angel Incarnate"*.

To Leonardo's second stay in Milan belongs a new version of the *Virgin of the Rocks* (now in London), displaying more decided sculptural-architectural effects than the former version, which for reasons still unclear was preferred by the clients to the Louvre painting. Lastly, there was the project for a new equestrian monument, this time dedicated to the Marshall of France Gian Giacomo Trivulzio, who intended to place it in his funeral chapel to be built in the Church of San Nazaro.

works is confirmed by some studies of drapery for the figure of the Virgin. In 1509, a year before beginning the *Saint Anne* panel, Leonardo painted another work, now also in the Louvre, the *St. John the Baptist*. It portrays a figure of disturbing aspect and gaze, smiling ambiguously, appearing as a mixture of the sacred and the profane due to the spirituality of the soft light that gently envelops the young body and, on the other hand, the sensuality of the features, which are the florid,

PAINTING, THE PREFERRED ART

For Leonardo painting, drawing, and music were activities which did not contrast with designing a machine or with engineering works, since for the Tuscan master art and science formed part of a single research into the intrinsic nature of things. Leonardo turned to the art of painting various times in his manuscripts, with comments, observations and notes in preparation for a treatise which he was never to complete. It was Francesco Melzi, his favorite pupil, who later collected, transcribed and arranged the material scattered through the codices he inherited at the master's death in 1519. The resulting work was the manuscript *Libro di pittura*, which was printed and published only in 1651, under the title *Trattato della pittura*. Leonardo was one of the first painters to use oil paints of Flemish origin in place of tempera. Among other reasons, this may be because oil paints, which dry more slowly, allowing corrections to be made even days later, were better suited to the artist's slow, methodic mode of working. As regards style, Leonardo's paintings are distinguished mainly by their sfumato, or soft shading, and their aerial perspective. Leonardo introduced the latter along with linear perspective – at the time a recent achievement, deemed indispensable in the Florentine painting milieu – to create a new way of rendering the perception of distant objects. No longer only through geometric solutions, in which distance was indicated by progressive decrease in size, but by a fine dosage of light and dark, of luminosity and shadow, which conveys

St. John the Baptist (c. 1509), Paris, Musée du Louvre.

Anonymous from Leonardo, **Angel of the Annunciation**, Basilea, Kunstmuseum.

the change in color and outlines of distant objects deriving from atmospheric effects. This effect was further enhanced by setting the figures in a landscape, as in the *Virgin of the Rocks*, preferred by Leonardo to scenes set in an interior, which instead facilitated the application of linear perspective. In similar manner, sfumato – with an effect like that achieved today in photography by so-called "soft-focus" images – indicates the volumes of the figures not with clear, sharp outlines and areas of decided color, but with soft transitions and shaded tones that seem to caress and veil the forms.

The date of the commission was probably after 1508, when drawings and studies for the sculpture were produced in succession, perhaps continuing in the years when the artist had moved to France. For Trivulzio, Leonardo revived the original idea for the Sforza Monument, of a rearing horse trampling a fallen enemy. In fact, given the size of the new monument, decidedly smaller than the one planned for the Sforza group, it seems likely that it could have been cast. However, this project too failed to be realized. A series of concomitant circumstances, the work on the chapel begun by Bramantino only after 1512, the death of Trivulzio in 1518 and then that of Leonardo the following year, brought this initiative to an end.

While during his second stay in Milan Leonardo's commitment to the artistic field is certain, it should be emphasized again that, in this period too, he worked above all on architectural projects and channeling initiatives. In the latter field new proposals were made, such as that for channeling the Adda River from Lecco to Milan, as well as plans for improving the existing network of canals. Of great importance are the hydrographic surveys of the Lombardy territory, from Lake Iseo to the Oglio River, from the Adda to the Tre Corni, to Trezzo and to Vaprio. In

Study for the equestrian monument
to Gian Giacomo Trivulzio
(c. 1508-1512),
Windsor (RL 12354).

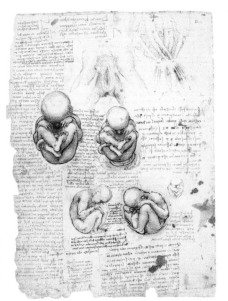

Female genitals
and fetus in the uterus
(c. 1510-1512),
Windsor (RL 19101).

lived, outside of the Western Gate. Of this project, planned between 1506 and 1508, there remain some sketches and notes, or brief descriptions, such as those of the banquet hall and the highly refined garden. For the latter the artist planned innumerable water tricks, fountains and automata, including the one designed to strike the hours of a gigantic water clock.

Lastly, important results were achieved by Leonardo in the field of anatomical studies. His great interest in the mysteries of the human body was further reinforced during these years by the practice of dissecting corpses, first described by the master in 1507-1508, as well as by the stimulating company of Marcantonio della Torre, physician and anatomist at the Studio di Pavia, with the aid of whom Leonardo carried out his studies. Moreover, the possibility of direct observation revolutionized anatomical illustration, until then rough and approximative, allowing Leonardo to execute anatomical plates that were both accurate and visually striking. Among the most famous drawings are the studies of the genital organs and those showing a fetus in its mother's uterus, taken it seems from the examination of a real human fetus of seven months which Leonardo had managed to obtain for dissection.

the latter locality was a villa owned by the family of Francesco Melzi, pupil and friend of the artist, who at the master's death was to inherit the codices. Here Leonardo spent long periods of sojourn and study.

Some architectural studies by the eclectic Tuscan are instead linked to the previously mentioned Charles d'Amboise. The governor of the Duchy of Milan, in fact, asked Leonardo to design for him a villa with garden to be built in the vicinity of the Church of San Babila, the district where the artist

THE YEARS IN ROME

The year of the Holy Alliance, invoked by Pope Julius II against the French, was 1511. The Pope's allies were Venice and Spain. Among the victorious results of the Alliance were, in 1512, the restoration of the Sforza family in Milan

moved to Rome, where had the support of Giuliano de' Medici, the Pope's brother. In Rome he lodged in the Vatican and had a studio at the Belvedere. But in the Papal city, whose splendor had been revived under Julius II, there was now only too much competition. Leonardo arrived when Michelangelo had just finished

and the return of the Medici to Florence, first with Giuliano, one of Lorenzo the Magnificent's sons, and then with Lorenzo, his grandson. Moreover, the Medici managed to attain the Papacy with the election of Cardinal Giovanni, another of Lorenzo's sons, as Pope under the name of Leo X in 1513. In Milan the position of Leonardo, linked to the French, became critical. In 1513 the artist painting the ceiling of the Sistine Chapel and Raphael the famous frescoes of the Stanze Vaticane. In Rome the master lived in isolation, dedicating himself to his various interests, from geometry to the study of waters – which found application in a project for draining the Pontine swamps and inspired around 1515 the first incredible drawings of the *Deluges*, which were to be continued during the years in France – to anatomical studies, conducted in the Hospital of Santo Spirito in 1514 and 1515, which were to provoke an accusation of sorcery subsequent to a denouncement made by one of his assistants. But this was not all. It was perhaps during these years that Leonardo began his most famous work, *La Gioconda* (or *Mona Lisa*), which was probably finished later in France. The Louvre *Bacchus* probably also dates from 1513-1519. An image similar to those of *St. John the Baptist* and the *Angel of the Annunciation*, its iconography may have been changed by the artist, due to the ambiguity emerging in the latter figures, from that of a sacred to that of a profane figure.

Rock wall collapsing under the weight of pounding rain (c. 1515), Windsor (RL 12380).

Raphael,
Portrait of Leo X between Cardinals Giulio de' Medici and Luigi de' Rossi
(1518-1519),
Florence, Uffizi Gallery.

Leonrdo and assistants
St. John the Baptist (Bacchus)
(c. 1513-1519),
Paris, Musée du Louvre.

**La Gioconda
(Mona Lisa)**
(c. 1513-1515),
Paris, Musée du Louvre.

Raphael,
Maddalena Doni
(c. 1506),
Florence, Palatine Gallery.

Raphael,
**Lady with
a Unicorn**
(c. 1506),
Rome, Galleria
Borghese.

In the previous pages:
**La Gioconda
(Mona Lisa)**
(c. 1513-1515), detail,
Paris, Musée du Louvre.

AT THE FRENCH COURT

Leonardo's, his stay in Rome was thus bitterly disappointing. As if this were not enough, in 1516 his protector, Giuliano de' Medici, died. It is thus unsurprising that in 1517 the master accepted the invitation of François I to move to France at his service. The king attributed him the highest honors, appointing him 'first painter, architect and engineer', offering him an excellent salary and lodging him in the Castle of Cloux, at the gates of Amboise, where the royal palace stood. Obviously, this was not merely a gilded exile. At the Court of François I, Leonardo was again a leading figure, assigned the usual important tasks that had marked his years in Italy.

As an artist, in France Leonardo gathered the fruits of his full maturity. It was in fact at Cloux that the unrivaled master probably completed his most famous painting, the *Mona Lisa*. On this world-famous work now in the Louvre, rivers of ink have flowed. Notwithstanding, Leonardo's panel is in many aspects still wrapped in mystery. First of all, the identity of the model is still unknown. Accepting the opinion of Vasari, who however never saw Leonardo's painting, it was long thought that the woman portrayed was the wife of the Florentine merchant Francesco del Giocondo,

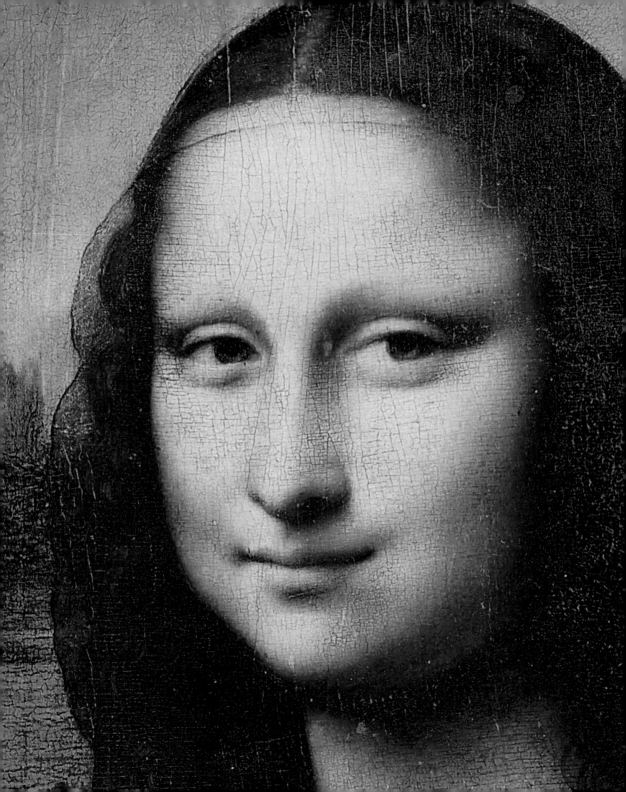

Mona Lisa Gherardini, whose husband commissioned the portrait.

This is the origin of the name *Gioconda*, as it was called by Cassiano dal Pozzo, convinced by reading Vasari, who saw the work at Fontainebleau in 1625.

For various reasons however, doubt has been cast on the identification of Leonardo's figure with the *Mona Lisa* of Vasari, a hypothesis now definitively rejected. Among these reasons is the testimony of Antonio de Beatis, secretary of Cardinal Louis d'Aragon, with whom he visited Leonardo at Cloux in 1517. De Beatis reports that during this visit the artist showed the Cardinal three paintings, of which one is undoubtedly the *Saint Anne* of the Louvre, another may be the *St. John* in the same museum, and the last is probably the *Mona Lisa*, which is described as follows: 'A certain Florentine lady, done from life, at the instance of the late Magnificent, Giuliano de Medici'. This means that, if the painting to which De Beatis refers is really the Louvre panel, the fact that it was painted for Giuliano de' Medici makes it highly improbable that it is a portrait of Francesco del Giocondo's wife, not to speak of the dating of the work, as will be seen.

But if she is not Mona Lisa, then who is the woman painted by Leonardo for the brother of Pope Leo X? Based

La Scapiliata (Portrait of a Girl) (c. 1508), Parma, Galleria Nazionale.

on the words of the Cardinal Louis d'Aragon's secretary, other conjectures have been made. Some experts have suggested Isabella Gualandi, a Neapolitan lady known to Giuliano. But the certainty of a name has never been attained. And along with those who have sought behind the ineffable smile of the *Mona Lisa* the reality of a historical personage – other

THE FRANCE OF FRANÇOIS I

François I, son of Charles d'Orléans Count of Angoulême and Luisa di Savoia, succeeded Louis XII, his father-in-law and distant relative, to the throne of France in 1515. During his reign the new King strengthened the prestige of the monarchy and improved the organization of the State. Determined to reinforce the power of the French throne, François I inaugurated an expansionist policy, managing to reconquer the Duchy of Milan within a year of becoming King. But his policy of conquest was destined to conflict with the power of Charles V, who, both for dynastic reasons and through coincidence, had managed to concentrate in his hands the Spanish throne (1516) and that of the Empire (1519), thus finding himself at the head of a reign of infinite extent (on which 'the sun never sets', as was said) which included the territories of the Hapsburgs and those of the Spanish crown. It was a dominion by which France felt itself particularly threatened, having become virtually encircled. François I thus had no choice but that of conflict with Charles V, in a long, hard and expensive struggle that continued almost up the death of the French King, shedding blood throughout Europe, with severe consequences for Italy. As regards the cultural life of his court François I, as a typical Renaissance sovereign of exquisitely humanist background, promoted literature and the arts, founding the Collège de France and calling to his service illustrious figures, among them Leonardo – who according to Vasari actually 'died in the arms of that King' – and Benvenuto Cellini, who made for him the famous gold Salt-cellar.

Jean Clouet,
François I
(c. 1525),
Paris, Musée du Louvre.

"candidates" are Costanza d'Avalos Duchess of Francavilla and Isabella d'Este – others have believed Leonardo's painting to be not the portrait of any real person but an ideal, symbolic likeness. A recent suggestion is that the painting is an allegorical representation of Chastity (the woman seated in a dominating position over the valley) who vanquishes Time (the mountainous landscape extending downward, eroded by the waters).

Other uncertainties concern the dating. Traditionally, the *Mona Lisa* is dated 1503-1506, at the time of the artist's second stay in Florence. This also depends on the fact that many scholars have seen the reflection of this extraordinary painting in the works of the young Raphael. In fact, an entirely "exterior" model of the iconographical type of the *Mona Lisa* had already been diffused in those years through other works by Leonardo, as shown by a painting such as the *Dama dei gelsomini* by Melozzo da Forlì. If in effect, as stated by De Beatis, the *Mona Lisa* was painted for Giuliano de' Medici, it may have been begun much later, probably around 1513-1515. And while it is true that in the early 16th century the artist could have met Giuliano in more than one place – for example in Venice in 1500 – he would certainly not have encountered him in Florence, where the Medici returned only in 1512 with the restoration of the family to power.

And a later dating of Leonardo's painting is suggested above all by questions of style. The subtle play of veils as well as the geological knowledge and misty atmosphere of the landscape admirably suspended in the distance evoke studies carried out after 1510: the previously mentioned drapery – black on black – for the painting of *Saint Anne* and the similar drawings at Windsor, dating from 1510-1511; or the landscapes of the Adda from 1513 and the others sketched in the margins of geometrical studies on sheets from 1514 and 1515. Appearing in close relationship with Leonardo's panel is a drawing made as late as around 1517-1518, known as the *Pointing Lady*, where the figure of a woman who resembles the *Mona Lisa* in her features, in her light dress and even in her smile, is portrayed in a landscape of rocks, water and plants immersed in mist, as she lifts a hand to point to something in the distance with a symbolic gesture. Lastly, what still perplexes the onlooker in the *Mona Lisa* is her mysterious smile. A smile that, as has been noted, exists in her eyes more than on her lips; that intense ex-

Volcanic explosion
(c. 1517),
Windsor (RL 12388).

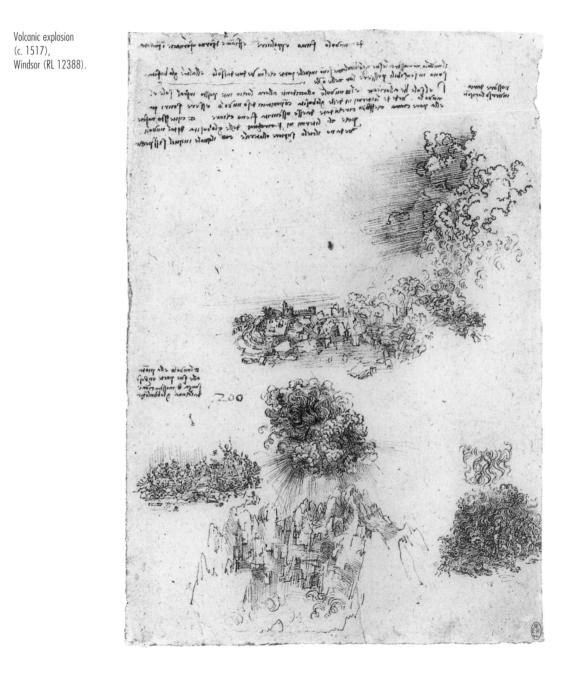

pression of the eyes and that curving mouth which also mark the Louvre *St. John*, another of the images that are disturbing since, as with the *Mona Lisa*, the onlooker feels himself in turn regarded.

The enigmatic smile of *Mona Lisa* has triggered ceaseless conjectures. Among the most fantastic are the ones that explain the strange expression lingering on her lips with reasons ranging from asthma, to blackening of the teeth caused by a mercury treatment against syphilis, to a hemiplegia of the model's left side, to bruxism, a disorder that causes the sufferer to grind his teeth during sleep or at times of stress. One hypothesis that may seem more likely is instead that the woman is pregnant, a situation that would also fit appropriately with the studies in embryology conducted by Leonardo in 1510-1513. According to a singular hypothesis advanced by Freud in a famous essay on the master of the Renaissance, the *Mona Lisa* may be an ideal portrait of the artist's mother. And still another doubt remains: the presence of a preparatory cartoon in which the figure of the *Gioconda* was nude. According to some scholars, this would explain the thinness of the modeling that distinguishes the painting and the various *Nude Giocondas* painted by followers and imitators. This having been said, if it is true

Pointing Lady
(c. 1517-1518),
Windsor (RL 12581).

Salai and Leonardo,
Nude Gioconda
(c. 1515).

School of Leonardo,
Nude Gioconda
(c. 1515),
St. Petersburg, Hermitage.

First reproduction
of the **Gioconda**
as illustration to a chapter
in the French edition of the
Trattato della pittura
by Leonardo (1651).

that during the years spent in France Leonardo soared freely to the highest spheres of art, it is also true that with the same naturalness and equal genius the master engaged, as in the past, in more superficial, transitory activities, such as festivals and performances. Already before settling in Cloux Leonardo had aroused a sensation in France with an amazing automaton, a "mechanical lion", fabricated in Florence and sent to Lyon in 1515 for the triumphal entry of François I crowned the new King of France. Then, after moving to France, in 1518 the master supervised the as-

tounding theatrical scenery designed to celebrate the presence of the King at Cloux, in imitation of the sets prepared for the famous Paradise Festival held years before in Milan. In the same year he designed the sets at Amboise that served as decoration for the baptism of the Dauphin and the wedding of Lorenzo de' Medici (nephew of Pope Leo X and future father of Caterina de' Medici Queen of France) and Maddalena de la Tour d'Auvergne, niece of François I. In addition to this, as always, the artist existed along with the technician and scientist. Continuing his studies carried out in Milan, Florence and Rome, in France as well Leonardo again turned his attention to the investigation of currents and whirlpools of water. Other projects for channeling rivers and draining land were devised, such as the one for channeling the Sologne and the plan for draining the swampy area around Romorantin. It was in this locality that the royal palace designed by Leonardo for the Queen Mother Luisa of Savoia, Countess of Angoulême, was to be built, with the artist again assuming the guise of architect. For the palace of Romorantin Leonardo's project was actually begun, but the malaria-infested area caused the work to be abandoned, so that the royal residence was built further to the north, at Chambord. Here the construction of the castle was begun in 1519, a few months after the death of Leonardo, but it is impossible to know whether and to what extent his drawings for Romorantin were utilized. The layout of the castle is quite simple; a linear scheme – recalling on the whole that of the Castello Sforzesco in Milan, well-known to him – on which however the artist planned a sort of residence-city, abounding in architectural solutions. And it is expressly in this dynamic development that lies the importance of Leonardo's project, in this study of a complex organism designed

to serve contemporaneously the functions of residence, entertainment and service. All this was to be achieved with the complicity of a system of running water serving for practical as well as aesthetic purposes (the pool for the naumachiae).

In April of 1519 Leonardo wrote his will. Perhaps he felt his last hour ap-

Old man seated on a rock and water studies
(c. 1513),
Windsor (RL 12579).

Allegory of navigation
(c. 1515),
Windsor (RL 12369).

The Chateau of Cloux (today Clos-Lucé), at Amboise, where Leonardo lived his last years, and the church of Saint-Florentin, where he was buried, in an early twentieth-century photo.

Jean-Auguste-Dominique Ingres,
François I receives the last breath of Leonardo da Vinci
(1818),
Paris, Musée du Petit Palais.

proaching. Already in 1517, at the time of the visit by Cardinal Louis d'Aragon, De Beatis had mentioned the hemiplegia that had struck his right side, certainly the source of suffering, although the artist was left-handed and could therefore still use his good hand. As executor of his will Leonardo appointed his friend and pupil Francesco Melzi, to whom he left all of his manuscripts and 'other instruments and devices'. The master asked to be buried in the Church of Saint-Florentin at Amboise.

The moment of his death, on May 2, 1519, was often imagined and depicted in paintings in the following centuries, the most famous of which is that of Ingres who, following the legend, showed Leonardo dying in the arms of François I in a scene rich in pathos, of typically romantic taste.

THE THEFT OF THE "MONA LISA"

Vincenzo Peruggia, who stole the **Mona Lisa** in 1911.

Incredible as it may seem, in the early 20th century the most famous painting in the world was stolen. It happened on a Sunday, August 20 of 1911. The Louvre was, as always, thronged with people, and then as now the crowds gathered especially in the Salon Carré to see the *Mona Lisa*, also known as *La Gioconda*. Among the visitors were three Italians, Vincenzo Peruggia and the two Lancellotti brothers. Peruggia had once worked in the museum, as one of the craftsmen commissioned to construct a showcase expressly designed to protect the *Mona Lisa*. Many copyists were always at work in the Louvre, regularly admitted to study and reproduce the museum's masterpieces. These artists kept their materials in a closet, so as not to have to bring them back and forth every day. And it was here that Vincenzo Peruggia and his accomplices hid overnight. The Louvre was in fact closed on Monday for maintenance. Early in the morning the three emerged from the closet, disguised as cleaners. At the right moment Peruggia headed for the Salon Carré, took down the *Mona Lisa* from the wall where it hung, aided by a series of favorable circumstances, and walked calmly out of the museum with the painting under his arm. Incredibly no one, until Tuesday afternoon, noticed the theft. This may seem impossible, but at the time paintings were often removed from the wall to be photographed or examined, and the absence of a work did not necessarily mean that it had been stolen. When the alarm was finally given, seventy inspectors and over a hundred gendarmes rushed to the Louvre. For a whole week this team scoured every corner of the museum, room by room, floor by floor. But by now *Mona Lisa* had taken flight. And this in spite of the fact that only the year before Théophile Homolle, Director of the French Museums, had declared: 'Steal the *Mona Lisa*? It's like thinking that someone could steal the tower of Notre-Dame Cathedral'. And yet it happened. The news of the theft shocked public opinion, blaring from the front pages of every newspaper. Who could have committed such an unthinkable crime? Someone who worked in the museum, a member of the cleaning crew or an underpaid custodian? Or even the directors of the Louvre themselves? A few heads fell, some were fired, suspended from work. But the *Mona Lisa* was not found. At the reopening of the Louvre a week later, a great crowd gathered as if for a funeral, swarming into the Salon Carré where everyone wanted to see the empty space on the wall left by the stolen painting, hung with a bunch of flowers brought by some unknown mourner. The outcry was so great that some who had never seen the painting itself went to see

Postcard commemorating the return of the **Mona Lisa** to the Louvre in 1914.

A satirical image inspired by the vicissitudes of the **Mona Lisa**, here brought back to France via Milan by Leonardo himself.

An image of the parade held in Paris in 1912 showing a **Mona Lisa** flying from the Louvre on an airplane.

where it had been taken away. There was a boom in souvenir postcards and the disappearance of *La Gioconda* give rise to an explosion of parodies, witticisms, and gags, in both theater and press. For two years the whereabouts of the famous painting were unknown. And the amazing joke is that it was only a few steps away from the Louvre, in the poor little apartment inhabited by Vincenzo Peruggia. But on whose behalf had the craftsman and his accomplices operated? Absurdly, even Picasso and the poet Apollinaire were suspected. It is possible instead that the theft was commissioned by a fifty-year-old Argentine, Eduardo de Valfierno, not a newcomer to the sale of counterfeit works of art. His purpose may have been that of selling at a high price six very faithful copies of the *Mona Lisa*, commissioned already before the theft with the complicity of the restorer Yves

Chaudron, to six American buyers convinced that they were purchasing the original. After which, Valfierno would no longer be interested in acquiring the real *Mona Lisa* from Peruggia. For this reason the painting remained in the hands of the Italian craftsman, who then decided to return to his native country where he would try to sell it. And so on December 10, 1913 Peruggia contacted a famous antiquarian, Alfredo Geri, in Florence, bringing him to his room in a hotel – later renamed Hôtel Gioconda – where he pulled out from under the bed a suitcase with Leonardo's masterpiece in it. Three days later Peruggia was arrested. At the trial he declared that he had acted only out of patriotism, wishing to bring the *Mona Lisa* back to the homeland of its artist. He got off with only about a year of imprisonment. *Mona Lisa* returned to her place in the Salon Carré of the Louvre on January 4, 1914.

The myth of Leonardo

Room of
**La Gioconda
(Mona Lisa),**
Paris, Musée du Louvre.

The back of the Italian
version of the 1 Euro coin
with a reproduction
of Leonardo's
Homo Vitruvianus.

A LEGEND IN HIS LIFETIME

Leonardo was a mythical figure already in his lifetime, like Michelangelo and Raphael. While he was still in Milan at the service of Ludovico il Moro, the court poet Bernardo Bellincioni celebrated his versatile genius by recalling the costumes and set designs he created for the famous Paradise Festival, held in 1490 to inaugurate the festivities for the wedding of Gian Galeazzo Sforza and Isabella d'Aragon. For this theatrical event of mythological theme, Bellincioni relates that 'with the great ingenuity and art of Maestro Leonardo da Vinci Florentine there was fabricated Paradise with all seven of the planets revolving in it, and the planets were represented by men'. And Leonardo appears again in Belloncioni's *Rime* of 1493, mentioned in an explanatory note beside the verse: 'From

Florence an Apelles has been brought here'. Such a comparison was superlative praise, placing the Tuscan master on the same level as the legendary artist from antiquity capable of painting "the invisible", one who was deemed the painter par excellence.

Another indication of the fame attained by Leonardo among his contemporaries is given by Bandello, who in one of his *Novelle* (Part I, Novella LVIII), published in 1554, recalls the great artist intent in working on the *Last Supper* in the Refectory of Santa Maria delle Grazie where 'some gentlemen [...] contemplated in silence the miraculous and most famous last supper of Christ with his Disciples, which the excellent painter Lionardo Vinci Florentine was then painting'. With the passage of time the fame and fortune of Leonardo have not diminished and today the genius from Vinci is more than ever a myth, to the point that it is difficult, if not impossible, to perceive his figure in a strictly philological sense. Over the centuries his image has become stratified, assuming characteristics which often have little to do with the real, historically existing personage. For example, some have viewed Leonardo as a "genius" in the romantic sense of the word, towering above his contemporaries in his diversity, exemplifying the supremacy and the tragedy of the individual. Others have thought him a forerunner of the positivist faith in progress, projected toward the future with his amazing inventions and his work as

Pieter Paul Rubens,
Grotesque drawing,
copy from Leonardo
(c. 1603),
Vienna, Albertina.

Giacomo Raffaelli,
Mosaic with
The Last Supper
(c. 1806-1814),
taken from a cartoon
by Giuseppe Bossi,
Vienna, Chiesa degli Italiani.

Andy Warhol,
The Last Supper.
Black/Green
(1986).

scientist, sweeping away Medieval superstition, freeing man from his age-old bonds. Others still venerate him as the author of that miraculous icon of modern times which the crowds flock to see in Paris, in a sort of secular pilgrimage. *La Gioconda*, or *Mona Lisa*, is in effect one of the cornerstones of the myth of Leonardo. Today – in the age of the technical reproducibility of works of art, to quote the words of Benjamin – the image of *Mona Lisa* has been exploited as never before, reproduced over and over in a wildly successful business to adorn everything from posters to T-shirts, from souvenirs to gadgets of all kinds.

FAMOUS INVENTIONS, BOTH TRUE AND FALSE

The famous drawing (false) of a "bicycle" which emerged during restoration of a folio from the Codex Atlanticus.

Studies on artificial flight (c. 1480), Codex Atlanticus (f. 1058).

Leonardo is known to all as a great inventor. However, practically none of the machines designed by him was actually built, or at least the only one to be documented is a water meter constructed around 1510 for the Florentine merchant and humanist Bernardo Rucellai. Among his projects, those which most struck the imagination of his contemporaries were machines that seem to have anticipated some great inventions of modern times. First among these was the flying machine. In the beginning it was an "ornithopter", a device designed to reproduce the beating wings of birds, driven by the strength of human muscles. Later, also through observation of the kites of the times, some of which were big enough to lift a man off the ground, Leonardo turned to something very similar to the modern hang glider, a machine designed to exploit air currents. Then there was the futuristic design for an aerial screw which actually looks like an ancestor of the helicopter. As regards Leonardo's flying machine, the story is still told of the unsuccessful attempt made by the young Zoroastro, who tested it by throwing himself from the top of Monte Ceceri, in the vicinity of Florence. But this is only a legend, which probably originated in a prophetic sentence written by Leonardo: 'The great bird will make its first flight from the top of Mount Cécero, filling the universe with amazement, filling with its fame all writings, and bringing eternal glory to the nest where it was hatched'. Other famous Leonardian studies are those on devices for breathing underwater, with drawings of rudimentary masks and diving bells;

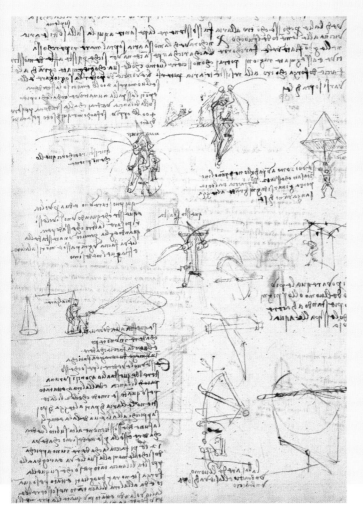

and of lifesavers. And the drawings of a submarine, an invention of which Leonardo himself wrote that he did not wish to divulge knowledge of it because it was potentially harmful to humanity. 'And this I will not publish nor divulge due to the evil nature of men'. In the Codex Atlanticus appear sketches of a self-propelled spring-operated vehicle, with three wheels and a steering wheel (a sort of automobile). In the Codex on the Flight of Birds, a device to protect the body from falls by the use of inflated wineskins is described – a prototype of the air-bag. Attributing Leonardo with having invented the first bicycle is instead decidedly false. This hypothesis was advanced on the basis of a drawing rediscovered in the Sixties during restoration of the Codex Atlanticus. And yet this too is a conviction firmly rooted in the popular imagination, as demonstrated by the souvenir T-shirts adorned with "Leonardo's bicycle" sold in the stalls of the famous Florentine market of San Lorenzo.

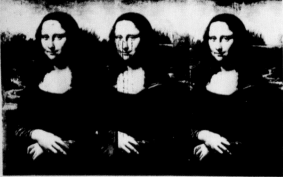

"MONA LISA" AS AN OBSESSION

Andy Warhol, **Mona Lisa (Colored)** (1963), detail.

On this work in particular the greatest attention has always been focused, beginning with the detailed description given by Vasari – although the 16th century writer had never seen the painting himself – who in his Lives even invented non-existent details, such as the eyelashes. But the *Mona Lisa* was to reach the peak of popularity in the 19th century, when there was a real explosion of "Leonadism". In the meantime, in 1800 Napoleon hung the painting – "Madame Lisa", as he liked to call it – in his bedchamber in the Tuileries Palace. Then in 1804 the work was moved to the Louvre. Its fame was thus definitively decreed, not merely because it could be seen by many more people but also because it was a work that, due to its aura of mystery and its ambiguous, androgynous nature, was bound to exert a strong attraction on the Romantic age and the following period of decadency. And while an artist such as Corot (*Portrait of a Lady with a Pearl*, 1868-1870) drew inspiration directly from the Leonardian model, it was primarily in the literary world that Mona Lisa was turned into a myth, by writers such as Théophile Gautier, Georges Sand, Joseph Péladan, Jean Lorraine and Jules Laforgue, as well as by Swinburne, Walter Pater and Oscar Wilde. Even Gabriele d'Annunzio – whose books included titles such as the *Virgin of the Rocks* and *Leda without a Swan* – wrote a tragedy entitled

Aimée Brune-Pages, **Leonardo as he paints the Gioconda** (1845), engraving by Charles Lemoine from the original painting, Paris, Bibliothèque Nationale.

FREUD AND LEONARDO

Even Sigmund Freud was fascinated by Leonardo. In 1910
the founder of psychoanalysis dedicated to the great artist
an essay in which he traced a debatable but indubitably
significant portrait. The brief passage reported here is taken
from a chapter in which Freud interpreted some of Leonardo's
adult behavior and mental attitudes as a reaction to his relationship
with his father during his childhood.

'Ma quel suo [di Leonardo] insegnare a spregiare l'autorità
e a respingere l'imitazione degli "antichi", quel suo non stancarsi
di indicare nello studio della natura la fonte di ogni verità,
ripetevano soltanto, nella forma più alta di sublimazione che sia
concessa all'uomo, la convinzione che già urgeva in lui bambino,
quando con stupore aveva aperto gli occhi sul mondo.
Ritradotti dall'astrazione scientifica nella concreta esperienza
individuale, gli antichi e l'autorità corrispondevano unicamente
al padre, e la natura ridiventava la tenera madre benigna che
l'aveva nutrito*'.

(This passage is taken from S. Freud, *Un ricordo d'infanzia di
Leonardo da Vinci*, in *Opere*, Turin 1974, vol. 6, pp. 207-285).

*'But his [Leonardo's] proclaiming that authority should be scorned
and imitation of the "ancients" abandoned, his ceaseless insistence
that the study of nature is the source of all truth, only repeated,
in the highest form of sublimation granted to man, the conviction
that had already arisen in him as a child, when with amazement he had
opened his eyes onto the world. Translated from scientific abstraction
into concrete individual experience, the ancients and authority only
represented his father, and nature became again the tender, benevolent
mother who had nourished him'.

Jean-Baptiste-Camille Corot,
**Portrait of a Lady
with a Pearl**
(1868-1870),
Paris, Musée du Louvre.

Terry Pastor,
Magritta Lisa
(1974).

Marcel Duchamp,
L. H. O. O. Q.
(1919).

La Gioconda in 1898. D'Annunzio, dedicating it moreover to 'Eleonora Duse of the beautiful hands', words which emphasize a decidedly Leonardian feature of the "divine" actress. As another proof of the immense fame of this painting, even a "popular" novelist such as Jules Verne wrote a play entitled *Mona Lisa* in 1874. But while it is true that the *Mona Lisa* has been idolized, it is also true that, like any object of excessive love, it has also been execrated. Against this cult image, become the symbol of Art with a capital A, the iconoclastic fury of the 20th century avant-garde was fiercely unleashed. The Futurists detested her. 'I see written on a wall in big white letters against a blue background: GIOCONDA ITALIAN LAXATIVE WATER. And under it the sickly-sweet face of Mona Lisa. Finally! At last even we are beginning to write good art criticism', wrote Ardengo Soffici in 1914, while Carrà called the painting 'fetid'. Desecrating images began to appear. In 1914 Malevič? "expunged" her face with two crisscross slashes and in 1919 Duchamp painted her with a moustache, creating the archetype of all future transgressive images of Leonardo's masterpiece. And even more, the inventor of the "ready-made" labeled his "revisitation" with an outrageous title, L.H.O.O.Q, letters that when read aloud in French sound like: 'Elle a chaud au cul [Her ass is burning]'. Duchamp's provocation was followed by

Chester Browton,
**A Chipp Off
the Old Block**
(1974).

Fernand Léger,
**Gioconda with Keys
(1930),**
Biot, Musée Fernand Léger.

Rita Greer,
Mona Lisamouse
(1977).

Rick Meyerowitz,
Mona Gorilla
(1971), poster.

many others, almost all irreverent, or at least using the image of *Mona Lisa* for an anti-conventional comment on art. These works ranged from a *Gioconda* by Dalí also adorned with a moustache, but this time identical to the one worn by the Spanish painter himself, to the *Gioconda with Keys* by Léger, to the "absent" sculpture (1967) by Magritte, to the even more recent "multiple" and "treated" *Giocondas* of Andy Warhol, and numerous other versions of the painting. Along with the *Mona Lisa*, another cult work of Leonardo's is the *Last Supper*, an equally famous painting whose fame has echoed down through the ages to our own time (as in the *Last Suppers* "revisited" by Andy Warhol), often treated in the same way as the *Mona Lisa*, although appearing less frequently. Widely known, often reproduced and "re-made" is also the *Homo Vitruvianus*, the drawing from 1490 from which Mario Ceroli has taken the sculpture that stands in the square in front of the *Museo Leonardiano di Vinci* and wich has, among other things, been engraved on the back of a Euro in the new European money. It was expressly to document the phenomenon of "Leonardism" that the Archivio Leonardismi was set up at Vinci in 1972. Since 1993 it has been a section of the *Museo Ideale di Vinci*, which through exhibitions and artefacts testifies to the undying vitality of the figure of Leonardo.

LEONARDO THE STAR

The myth of Leonardo has been celebrated not only in art and literature but also in the cinema, where interest in the eclectic Renaissance artist has recently shifted mainly to the personage, to his human dimension, as in the successful biographical TV film by Renato Castellani *The Life of Leonardo da Vinci*, from 1971. Crucial scenes in the film story are those where Leonardo impassibly confronts the reality of death, as when he draws one of the hanged men condemned in the Pazzi Conspiracy of 1478, or when he dissects cadavers in the Florentine Hospital of Santa Maria Nuova. These are exemplary scenes, through which the director communicates the driving urge that animated the great master's thirst for knowledge, going beyond any moral scruple. This brings to mind a passage from Freud's essay on Leonardo, in which the Viennese psychoanalyst notes that the artist – like an ante litteram pacifist and animal-rights agitator – 'was gentle and benevolent with all; refused, it seems, to eat meat, since he deemed it unjust to deprive animals of life, and found a singular pleasure in setting free birds that he had bought at the market. He condemned war and bloodshed and called man not so much the "king of animals" as "the first beast among animals". But', continued Freud, 'this feminine delicacy of feeling did not prevent him from accompanying criminals condemned to death to the execution place, in order to study the anguished expressions on their faces and to draw them in his notebook. It did not prevent him from designing the most atrocious offensive weapons and putting himself at the service of Cesare Borgia in the capacity of supreme military engineer. Often he seemed indifferent to good and evil'. Another film in which Leonardo appears is *Non ci resta che piangere* by Roberto Benigni and Massimo Troisi (1984).

Philippe Leroy playing Leonardo in the televised **Life of Leonardo** (1971) by Renato Castellani.

The actor Fëdor Šaljapin,
interprets Leonardo,
in the film
I sovversivi (1967)
by the Taviani brothers.

Leonardo, Ludovico il Moro
and Cecilia Gallerani in
a scene from the televised
Life of Leonardo
(1971)
by Renato Castellani.

THE FICTIONAL LEONARDO

Leonardo da Vinci or the Resurrection of the Gods is a novel
by the Russian author Dmitrij Sergeevič Merežkovskij, published
in 1901. The work forms part of a trilogy of novels entitled *Christ
and Anti-Christ*, each of which focuses on the life of a famous
historical personage. The great artist of the Renaissance is the hero
of the second volume; the most problematical of the Roman
emperors that of the first, *Julian the Apostate* or *The Death of the
Gods* (1896). Lastly, Tsar Peter the Great is the central figure
of the third, *Peter and Alexis or the Anti-Christ* (1905). In the
book dedicated to Leonardo, Merežkovskij traces a fascinating
biography of the supreme artist, interweaving history and fantasy
in a vivid retelling of the most significant moments in the life and
work of this personage who has become legendary.
Memorable among the many stirring passages in the book is
the one in the chapter called the *Diary of Giovanni Boltraffio*,
where the author pretends to report the comments made by one
of Leonardo's best-known pupils on his personal experience at the
master's side. The action takes place in Milan, where Leonardo
is working on the Last Supper: 'Osservo come lavora attorno
alla Santa Cena. Alla mattina presto, appena sorto il sole, esce
di casa e se ne va al convento; per tutta la giornata, fin quasi
al crepuscolo, rimane a dipingere, dimenticandosi persino di
mangiare. Qualche volta invece passano intere settimane senza che
si decida a riprendere i pennelli. Però ogni giorno per due o tre
ore se ne rimane ritto davanti al dipinto, a esaminare, soppesare
e meditare il lavoro compiuto. Talvolta, in pieno mezzogiorno,
interrompe bruscamente un lavoro cominciato, per precipitarsi al
convento, correndo quasi per le vie deserte senza neppur ripararsi
all'ombra dal sole cocente, come spinto da una strana irresistibile
forza; e giunto al convento sale sull'impalcatura, afferra i pennelli,
dà due o tre rapidi tocchi al quadro e se ne ritorna rapidamente

a casa. In questi ultimi giorni il maestro ha lavorato alla testa dell'apostolo Giovanni. Voleva, a quanto ha detto, finirla proprio oggi; invece con mio grandissimo stupore, non si è mosso da casa e fin dal mattino si è messo [...] a osservare il volo dei calabroni, delle vespe e delle mosche. È talmente immerso nello studio della struttura dei loro corpi e delle loro ali, che si direbbe ne dipendano le sorti dell'universo. Ha toccato le vette della felicità avendo scoperto che le zampette posteriori delle mosche servono anch'esse da timone di direzione: a suo parere, tale scoperta è enormemente preziosa e utile alla costruzione della sua macchina per volare. Può darsi benissimo, ma è tuttavia spiacevole pensare che la testa dell'apostolo Giovanni sia rimasta incompiuta anche oggi, per l'osservazione delle zampette delle mosche'*. (This passage is taken from D. S. Merežkovskij, *Leonardo da Vinci*, Giunti, Florence 1998).

In 2003 the American author Dan Brown published *The da Vinci Code*. It immediately became a record-breaking international bestseller and was made into a film in 2006. The novel was scathingly reviewed by the critics and even more strongly criticized by the Catholic hierarchies for its numerous historical errors, potentially subversive in the light they cast on Christianity and the Church of Rome. In this book, several paintings by Leonardo are mentioned (*The Last Supper*, *The Virgin of the Rocks*, *Mona Lisa*). Skilfully interwoven with the unfolding of the plot and with the author's thesis, these paintings play a crucial role in the novel. As regards *The Last Supper* in particular, Dan Brown boldly challenges the official opinion of art historians by declaring that the figure of the apostle John is in reality Mary Magdalene, believed to be, based on the apocryphal Book of Philip, not merely the repentant sinner who asked for and was granted pardon by Christ, but actually the wife of Jesus.

*'I observe how he works on the *Holy Supper*. In the early morning, as soon as the sun has risen, he leaves his house and goes to the monastery. All day long, until nearly sunset, he stays there painting, even forgetting to eat. Sometimes instead he spends whole weeks without deciding to pick up his brushes again. But every day, for two or three hours, he stands in front of the painting, to examine it, assess it and meditate on the work he has done. Sometimes, at the height of noon, he abruptly interrupts some work he has begun to hurry to the monastery, almost running through the deserted streets without even trying to take shelter from the burning sun, as if urged on by an uncanny, irresistible force. And having reach the monastery he climbs onto the scaffolding, grasps the brushes, gives two or three rapid touches to the painting and quickly returns home. In the last few days the master has worked on the head of the Apostle John. He wanted, he said, to finish it just today; instead to my very great amazement, he has not left the house, and since morning he has been occupied [...] in observing the flight of yellow jackets, wasps and flies. He is so deeply immersed in studying the structure of their bodies and wings, that you would think the fate of the universe depended on it. He was in seventh heaven to discover that flies use their hind legs as a rudder for changing direction. In his opinion, this discovery is enormously important and useful to the construction of his flying machine. This may very well be, but it is sad to think that the head of the Apostle John has remained unfinished again today, since the master preferred to observe the legs of flies'.

Representation of
Last Supper
Leonardo's in the film
Viridiana (1961)
by Luis Buñuel.

Leonardo
(Patrick Godfrey)
and Cinderella
(Drew Barrymore)
in **The Legend
of a Love** (1998)
by Andy Tennant.

Bruno Barnabè playing
Leonardo, in a scene
from the film **The Last
Supper** (1950)
by Luigi Giachino.

Here the accent is placed chiefly on Leonardo the scientist and inventor, another of the most famous and revered aspects of the Tuscan master over the centuries. But in this case the tone is decidedly satirical. The heroes of the film, having ended up by some strange chance back in the year 1492 (in historical reality, Leonardo was in Milan, at the court of "il Moro", that year), meet the artist, whose features are those, now become a cliché, of the famous (supposed) *Self-portrait* of Turin. Leonardo is standing on the banks of a river, obviously busy with one of his inventions, a hydraulic machine resembling one of those actually to be seen in his drawings. In an irresistibly funny gag, the heroes try to take advantage of the fantastic chance of having met the great inventor. They hope with his assistance to build machines from the future, so as to win glory and wealth. First they try to explain to Leonardo the functioning of the train, then of the thermometer. But in vain; Leonardo is a great disappointment to them, he remains perplexed, seems to have understood nothing. The two walk away disconsolate, annoyed at having believed in the genius of a personage evidently overestimated by history. But they are convinced of Leonardo's genius in the end, when the master triumphantly appears driving a steam-engine train, which he has somehow managed to invent on the basis of the confused indications given by his two friends "come from the future".

This farcical Leonardo, in whom converge all of the trite commonplaces linked to the personage, is a final proof of the well-consolidated myth that justly surrounds a figure so complex and fascinating in the history of humanity.

Cronology

At Arezzo, in the Church of San Francesco, Piero della Francesca begins the cycle of frescoes known as the *Legend of the True Cross*.	1452	Leonardo is born at Vinci on April 15, the natural son of the notary Ser Piero di Antonio da Vinci.
	1469	Leonardo presumably enters Verrocchio's workshop in this year.
	1472	He is enrolled in the painters' association, the Compagnia di San Luca. His first works start from this date: costumes and sets for festivals and jousts, a cartoon for a tapestry (lost) and the paintings of uncertain dating.
	1473	He dates (August 5) the drawing of the *Landscape with the view Val d'Arno* (Florence, Uffizi Gallery, GDS).
In Milan, Galeazzo Maria Sforza is assassinated in a conspiracy. He is succeeded by his son Gian Galeazzo.	1476	Accused of sodomy along with other persons, he is acquitted.
The Pazzi conspiracy, fomented by Pope Sixtus IV, fails. Giuliano de' Medici is killed, but the authority of his brother, Lorenzo the Magnificent, is reinforced.	1478	Leonardo is commissioned to paint the altarpiece for the Chapel of San Bernardo in Palazzo della Signoria. He states that he has completed two paintings of the Virgin, one of which is now identified as the *Benois Madonna*.
Ludovico Sforza imprisons his nephew and illicitly becomes the lord of Milan.	1480	According to the Anonimo Gaddiano, Leonardo works for Lorenzo de' Medici.
	1481	Contract for the *Adoration of the Magi*.
	1482	Leonardo moves to Milan leaving unfinished the *Adoration*.
Raphael is born in Urbino.	1483	In Milan he stipulates the contract for the *Virgin of the Rocks* with Evangelista and Ambrogio de' Predis.
	1487	Payment for projects for the lantern on the Milan Cathedral.
	1489	Leonardo designs sets for the festivities celebrating the wedding of Gian Galeazzo Sforza and Isabella d'Aragon. In this same year he begins preparations for the colossal equestrian statue in honor of Francesco Sforza.
In Florence, Lorenzo de' Medici dies. The system of alliances sanctioned by the Peace of Lodi begins to break up.	1492	For the wedding of Ludovico il Moro and Beatrice d'Este, Leonardo designs the costumes for the procession of Scythians and Tartars.
The King of France Charles VIII allies himself with Ludovico il Moro, invades Italy and claims his right to the Kingdom of Naples.	1494	Land reclamation work on one of the Duke's estates near Vigevano.
	1495	Leonardo begins *The Last Supper* and the decoration of rooms in the Castello Sforzesco. The artist's name is mentioned as Ducal Engineer.
	1497	The Duke of Milan urges the artist to finish *The Last Supper*, which is probably completed by the end of the year.
Michelangelo is commissioned to sculpt the *Pietà* for St. Peters. In Florence Savonarola is burned at the stake.	1498	Leonardo completes the decoration of the Sala delle Asse in the Castello Sforzesco.

	Year	
Luca Signorelli begins the frescoes for the Chapel of San Brizio in the Orvieto Cathedral. Milan is occupied by the King of France Louis XII.	1499	Leonardo leaves Milan with Luca Pacioli. He stops at Vaprio to the Melzi family, then leaves for Venice passing through Mantua, where he draws two portraits of Isabella d'Este.
In Florence, Piero di Cosimo paints the *Stories of Primitive Humanity*.	1500	In March he arrives in Venice; returns to Florence where he resides at the Monastery of the Servite Brothers in SS. Annunziata.
In Rome, Bramante begins the Tempietto di San Pietro in Montorio and the Belvedere Courtyard.	1502	Leonardo enters the service of Cesare Borgia as architect and general engineer, following Borgia in his military campaigns through Romagna.
	1503	Leonardo returns to Florence where, according to Vasari, he paints the *Mona Lisa*. Devises projects for deviating the Arno River during the siege of Pisa. Commissioned by the Signoria to paint the *Battle of Anghiari*.
Michelangelo finishes the *David* commissioned three years before by the Republic of Florence. Raphael paints the *Marriage of the Virgin*, then moves to Florence, where he is influenced by the work of Leonardo.	1504	Continues to work on the *Battle of Anghiari*. Is called upon to participate in the commission that will decide where to place Michelangelo's *David*. First studies for a Leda.
	1506	Leonardo leaves Florence for Milan, promising to return within three months. The stay in Milan extends beyond this time.
In Rome Michelangelo begins frescoing the ceiling of the Sistine Chapel. In Venice, Giorgione and Titian fresco the Fondaco dei Tedeschi.	1508	Leonardo is in Florence, then returns to Milan.
Raphael is in Rome, where he begins decorating the Stanze Vaticane.	1509	Geological studies on the valleys of Lombardy.
	1510	Studies on anatomy with Marcantonio della Torre at the University of Pavia.
Michelangelo completes the frescoes on the ceiling of the Sistine Chapel. The Sforza family returns to Milan.	1512	
Julius II dies. He is succeeded by Giovanni de' Medici (Leo X). In Florence, Andrea del Sarto begins the frescoes known as *Stories of the Virgin*.	1513	Leonardo leaves Milan for Rome, where he lives in the Vatican Belvedere, under the protection of Giuliano de' Medici. Remains in the city for three years, engaged in mathematical and scientific studies and projects for draining the Pontine swamps and for the port of Civitavecchia.
In Rome, Raphael and his assistants paint the Vatican Loggias and the Psyche Loggia in the Villa Farnesina.	1517	Leonardo moves to Amboise, to the court of François I King of France. In mid-January he visits Romorantin with the King to plan a new royal palace and a system of canals for the region of Sologne.
	1518	Leonardo participates in the festivities for the baptism of the Dauphin and for the wedding of Lorenzo de' Medici to the King's niece.
Charles V of Hapsburg is elected Emperor of the Holy Roman Empire; open conflict breaks out between France and the Empire. In Parma, Correggio paints the Camera della Badessa in the convent of San Paolo.	1519	On April 23 Leonardo writes his will. The executor is his friend the painter Francesco Melzi. He dies on May 2. In the burial certificate, dated August 12, he is described as a 'noble Milanese, first painter and engineer and architect to the King, State Mechanic'.

Index

The numbers in **bold** refer to the illustrations

Bibliography

Works of general nature: The enormous bibliography on Leonardo has been collected in the twenty volumes of the *Raccolta Vinciana* (Milan 1905-1964) and in the *Bibliografia Vinciana*, edited by E. Verga (Bologna 1931), supplemented with an article by Ludwig H. Heydenreich in the "Zeitschrift für bildende Kunst", 1935. Still in the bibliographical field, more recent is the contribution of A. Lorenzi and P. Marani with the *Bibliografia Vinciana 1964-1979* (1979-1982). To Leonardo the architect, L. H. Heydenreich has dedicated a large part of his studies. More recent is the *Leonardo Architetto* by C. Pedretti (Milan 1988). For an overview of Florentine art at the time of Leonardo, see A. Chastel, *Arte e Umanesimo a Firenze al tempo di Lorenzo il Magnifico. Studi sul Rinascimento e sull'Umanesimo platonico* (Turin 1964); W. AA., *Leonardo. la pittura*, Florence 1985; P. Marani, *Il Cenacolo di Leonardo*, Milan 1986; P. Marani, *Leonardo. Catalogo completo dei dipinti*, Florence 1989; J. Shell, *Leonardo*, London-Paris 1992; M. Cianchi, *Leonardo*, Florence 1996; W. AA., *Il Cenacolo*, Milan 1999; C. Pedretti, *Leonardo. Le macchine*, Florence 1999; W. AA., *Leonardo. Arte e scienza*, Florence 2000; C. Pedretti, S. Taglialagamba, *Leonardo. L'arte del disegno*, Florence 2014; F. Zöllner, N. Johannes, *Leonardo da Vinci. I disegni*, Cologne 2014; P. C. Marani, M. T. Fiorio (ed. by), *Leonardo da Vinci. 1452-1519. Il disegno nel mondo*, Milan 2015.

Studies on the codices: Useful compendiums cataloguing the contents and dates of the individual codices and the manuscript folios dispersed in various collections are found in the two-volume anthology by J.-P. Richter, *The Literary Works of Leonardo da Vinci*, London 1883 and Oxford 1939, updated by another two volumes by C. Pedretti, *Commentary*, Oxford 1977. Specialized studies on the codices include that of G. Calvi, *I manoscritti di Leonardo da Vinci dal punto di vista cronologico, storico e biografico*, Bologna 1925, while the often adventurous aspects of their history have been described by several scholars on various occasions, especially in the introductions to the facsimile editions, for which reference should be made to the above-mentioned bibliography by Verga. A contextual view of the vicissitudes and the nature of the codices is given in the fundamentally important contribution of A. Marinoni, *I manoscritti di Leonardo da Vinci e le loro edizioni*, in *Leonardo. Saggi e ricerche*, Rome 1954, pp. 229-263. Marinoni is also responsible for the monumental edition of the Codex Atlanticus, of the French manuscripts and of other codices published in facsimile by Giunti of Florence within the context of the program for the National Edition of Leonardo's works. Two major contributions from abroad have been made by the Elmer Belt Library of Vinciana at the University of California di Los Angeles: E. Belt - K. T. Steinitz, *Manuscripts of Leonardo da Vinci. Their History, with a Description of the Manuscript Editions in Facsimile*, Los Angeles 1948 and K. T. Steinitz, *Bibliography of Leonardo da Vinci's Treatise on Painting*, Copenhagen 1958. The codices which contain studies on architecture (and thus almost all of them) are reviewed in a book by C. Pedretti, *Leonardo da Vinci. The Royal Palace at Romorantin*, Cambridge (Mass. 1972), pp. 138-147. The first document on the dispersion of Leonardo's papers kept in the 16th century at the Villa Melzi at Vaprio d'Adda appears in the *Memorie di don Ambrogio Mazenta* published in a critical edition and with facsimile by L. Gramatica in 1919.

For the history of the manuscripts before their dispersion, and thus containing hitherto unknown aspects of the diffusion of Leonardo's ideas, reference should be made to the edition by C. Pedretti and C. Vecce of the *Libro di Pittura* compiled on the basis of Leonardo's manuscripts by his pupil and heir Francesco Melzi, published for the first time in facsimile within the context of the Vincian program of the Giunti publishing house (1995).

On the drawings: The first study of Leonardo's drawings with annotated catalogue was made by B. Berenson, *The Drawings of the Florentine Painters*, London 1906, extended and revised in the subsequent editions of (1938) and in that of Milan (1961). Fundamentally important are the studies of A. E. Popp, *Leonardo Zeichnungen* (1928), reassumed by K. Clark in his catalogue of the Windsor Collection, published at Cambridge (1935), revised and extended with the assistance of C. Pedretti (London 1968-1969). Clark also had the idea for a catalogue of all of Leonardo's drawings, realized by A. E. Popham, *The Drawings of Leonardo da Vinci*, London 1946. Starting from 1957 are the contributions of C. Pedretti: *Leonardo da Vinci. Fragments at Windsor Castle from the "Codex Atlanticus"*, London 1957; the catalogue of the folios in the Codex Atlanticus after its restoration (Florence and New York 1978-1979), and the facsimile edition of the Windsor Collection, of which the following had already been published: the corpus of the Anatomical Studies (1978-1979), that of the Studies on Nature (1982) and the Studies of Horses (1984), in a program carried out for the Italian edition by Giunti. To these works has now been added the series containing facsimiles of Leonardo's dispersed drawings and those of his school now in various collections.

PHOTOGRAPHS
Giunti Archives/ Foto Rabatti & Domingie: 2, 52, 54, 56, 60a, 61, 62-63, 64, 65, 66, 91, 115, 123a; Giunti Archives/Massimo Borchi: 9c, 11; Archivio Storico del Cinema/AFE: 149a, 152, 153; By permission of the Ministero per i Beni e le Attività Culturali: 84, 85, 86, 87; Archivi Alinari: 69, 123b; Massimo Borchi/Atlantide: 12a, 14a; Guido Cozzi/Atlantide: 12b; John Haseltine/Corbis: 8; Robert Holmes/Corbis: 136; Erich Lessing/Contrasto: 89b; Antonio Quattrone, Florence: 51b, 76, 77, 103, 117; Rabatti & Domingie, Florence: 88. Leonardo's drawings are taken from the Edizione Nazionale dei Manoscritti e dei disegni di Leonardo da Vinci, Giunti Editore. Photographs not listed here are from the Giunti Archives. Works found the Italian State Galleries are reproduced by permission of the Ministero per i Beni e le Attività Culturali. © Succession Marcel Duchamp, by SIAE 2017; © Fernand Léger, by SIAE 2017; © Andy Warhol Foundation for the Visual Arts, by SIAE 2017.
The publisher is prepared to meet all copyright obligations pertinent to photographs whose sources could not be ascertained.

Printed by
Lito Terrazzi s.r.l.
Stabilimento di Iolo